ENTERTAINING
AT HOME
IN SCOTLAND

ENTERTAINING AT HOME IN SCOTLAND

SUE LAWRENCE

The Winner of BBC Masterchef 1991

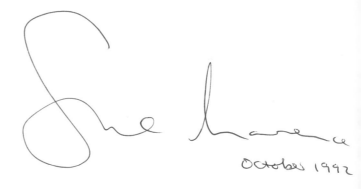

October 1992

MAINSTREAM
PUBLISHING

EDINBURGH AND LONDON

First published in Great Britain 1992 by
MAINSTREAM PUBLISHING COMPANY (EDINBURGH)
LTD
7 Albany Street
Edinburgh EH1 3UG

ISBN 1 85158 409 9

A catalogue record for this book is available from the
British Library

Typeset in Baskerville by Blackpool Typesetting Services
Ltd, Blackpool

Printed by Mandarin Offset Ltd, Hong Kong

Photography by Victor Albrow

Calligraphy by Joi Lynda Millgate

Design by James Hutcheson

To Pat, for being an uncomplaining guinea-pig.

Contents

Acknowledgments

My thanks extend to each of the 12 chefs who kindly contributed a recipe; to Hils for recipe testing; and to Anne for helping with food styling. Also to Jenners, Edinburgh, for providing crockery, cutlery and material for the photography; to Anta (made in Scotland) for the ceramic tartan plates; to Robert Wilson of Scotherbs, Errol, for supplying his superb herbs; to Ian Breslin of Armstrongs, Raeburn Place, Edinburgh, for providing his wonderful seafood; and to my favourite delicatessen, Herby's of Raeburn Place, for their provisions. I am particularly grateful to my parents for their constant support – and baby-sitting!

Notes on Measurements and Serving Numbers

Metric and Imperial measurements have been given to their nearest rounded equivalent. Results will be satisfactory only when one set of measurements is adhered to. To use American or Australian cup measurements, an approximate conversion is: 1 cup to 250 ml (8 fl oz).

Unless otherwise stated, all my recipes serve four. In the chefs' recipes, the serving number is individually specified.

Introduction

SCOTLAND HAS, WITHOUT DOUBT, ONE OF THE BEST LARDERS IN THE world. Where else could you find top-quality game, beef, lamb, fish, shellfish, soft fruits, wild mushrooms, barley, oats – all in abundance. Yet Scots in the past seemed oblivious of the splendid produce on their doorstep. Consequently, they have allowed much of it, particularly seafood, to be exported. In the last couple of decades, however, Scotland's culinary cornucopia has been increasingly appreciated, not only by visitors, but also by the Scots themselves. This change has been inspired by a growing band of Scottish chefs and restaurateurs, who have elevated plain Scottish 'cooking' to the levels of *haute cuisine*.

Good, plain Scottish dishes like mince and tatties, soups and the best of baking were the staples of my youth. Then, food was eaten almost exclusively for sustenance. Guests were invited for hearty lunches or teas, but not for dinner – an unknown concept which smacked of southern decadence. Nevertheless, whatever the occasion, whether visitors were invited or just popping in, they were always made to feel extremely welcome. The warmth of Scottish hospitality has not changed an iota, but the style of entertaining has. More and more people prefer to have guests in the evening, which is concordant with the increase in popularity of wine-drinking; 'tea' is essentially a meal which is accompanied by a cup of tea. By delaying the hour of eating and by offering wine, there has been a gradual move towards dinner-party or supper-party entertaining in Scotland. Coupled with the upsurge of new, exciting restaurants and the plethora of cookery books from the 1970s onwards, there is now a growing interest in more sophisticated forms of cooking.

Despite the advance of these ambitious culinary styles, the 'basics' have not been forgotten, and indeed, some have been rediscovered. Oyster or mussel stew used to be everyday fare in Scotland until the end of the last century. Now these molluscs, which are not as expensive as some may imagine, are regaining their popularity. There is no finer taste of the sea than freshly bought and simply prepared oysters. In my recipes, I have incorporated some old favourites – for example, stovies, skirlie, gingerbread – into recipes for the 1990s. Health is a major issue nowadays and this is reflected in a minimal use of butter, cream, flour-enriched sauces or fatty cuts of meat. My personal partiality for salads means there are many raw vegetable accompaniments. The occasional indulgent pudding, like pecan pie or 7-cup pudding, are aberrations which my sweet tooth insists upon.

My own style of cooking evolved from my Dundee University days in the mid-1970s. Hitherto, I had learned the Scottish basics from my mother – scones, pancakes, broth, mince, rumbledethumps. In shared flats at university, experimentation began in earnest. We began cooking 'adventurous' dishes like curries, lasagnes and spaghetti bolognaise. My year in France, in the Pyrenees, plus a summer as an au pair in Provence, opened my eyes to true gastronomy. Whether I sat at the magnificent school lunches or in a family's home, the French attitude towards food impressed me greatly – people actually discussed a dish's finer points. Scots on the whole were not used to such frivolous chat; I still wonder how Robert Burns got away with it in his address, *To a Haggis!*

Back at university, I was able to visit two of the fine restaurants in Fife, which were gaining popularity – The Peat Inn and The Grange Inn – spending half of my grant in a night; but it was, after all, educational! My passion for food had begun, and continued after marrying, in 1981, and becoming a Forces wife. Entertaining was *de rigueur*, so I launched into the role of hostess with relish. Our first three years of married life, on a German Air Force base, involved numerous squadron detachments. During these absences, my salvation was Hils, the other British wife. She inspired me to greater culinary achievements, through her own cooking skills.

In 1989 my husband left the Forces and we moved back to my home town of Edinburgh. There, probably for the first time, I became aware of the potential of Scottish food. Also, I found a much greater range of foreign foods available in the shops than there had been eight years earlier. So I began creating dishes which combined the best of Scottish produce with ingredients I had discovered in my travels (besides France and Germany, I have lived in Finland and Australia).

My recipes are simple, for with such good-quality ingredients, I see no need to mask natural flavours. Balancing a menu was something which struck me as extremely significant, in the two competitions I won: The Sunday Times Scotland Amateur Chef of the Year in 1990 and BBC Masterchef in 1991. I have, therefore, devised a full menu for each chapter, although the recipes are obviously interchangeable. Balance not only involves texture, lightness and colour, but also money: a cheap starter means you can afford to pay more for the main course or pudding.

I have been fortunate, since winning the Masterchef title, to have written a series of articles for *The Scotsman*, interviewing top chefs in Scotland. I found them all interesting, personable characters, who are passionate in wanting to reflect their area by using the best of local produce in their cooking. I am indebted to the 12 chefs who kindly contributed a recipe to this book.

Trying to sum up the style of my book is not easy: eclectic, hopefully innovative, but essentially simple – it is a celebration of some of Scotland's abundant natural larder. The underlying theme is the use of not necessarily expensive, but certainly top-quality ingredients. Also, there is a blend of the traditional or even ordinary with the more unusual or exotic. Edward Lear anticipated my tastes with the improbable combination served at the owl and the pussy-cat's nuptial feast:

'They dined on mince and slices of quince
Which they ate with a runcible spoon.'

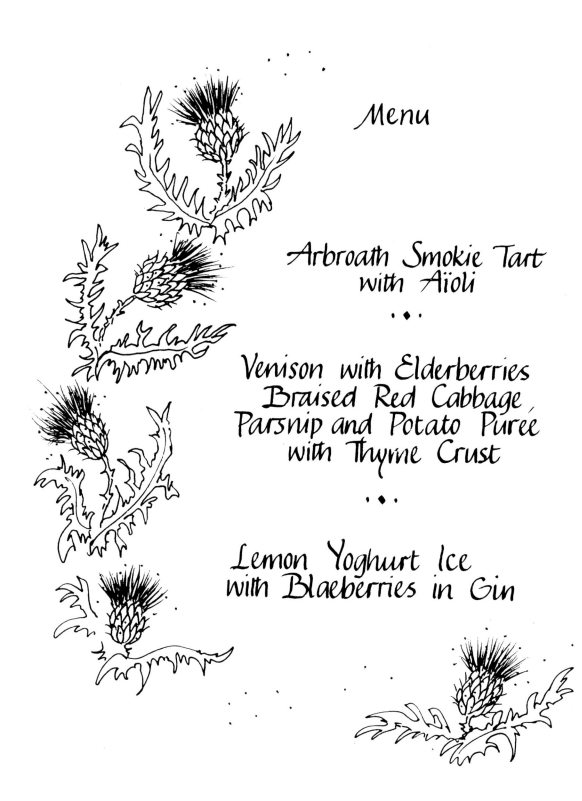

Menu

**Arbroath Smokie Tart
with Aïoli**

• •

**Venison with Elderberries
Braised Red Cabbage
Parsnip and Potato Purée
with Thyme Crust**

• •

**Lemon Yoghurt Ice
with Blaeberries in Gin**

Chapter One

THIS MENU INCORPORATES SOME ARCHETYPAL SCOTTISH FLAVOURS. Arbroath smokies are a great favourite of mine: I always buy them, and also crab, when I visit my sister, who lives in Arbroath. A good way to flake the fish is to warm them in a low oven for 10 minutes (or a microwave for 4 minutes), which loosens the skin. Once this is removed, carefully flake the flesh, avoiding the small bones. Smokies are ideal for crêpes, mousses and pâtés, or simply served cold with a green salad and baked potato. The aïoli, to accompany the tart, has less garlic cloves than the southern French equivalent, so the pungency of the garlic does not overpower the delectable flavour of the smokies. Aïoli is essentially a garlic mayonnaise and it is very easy to make in the food processor. I would recommend using a good quality olive oil, preferably extra virgin – I prefer Italian to Spanish.

The venison I use for the main course is farmed red deer; its flavour is excellent as it is well hung. During the open season (in Scotland 21 October to 31 March for roe does) fillet of wild roe deer is also superb. Venison is a very lean meat – the fillet has virtually no fat at all. Therefore, great care must be taken not to over-cook the meat, or it will dry out. To make the stock, ideally use venison bones. If you buy from a deer farm, they should sell them to you; I buy mine from Fletcher's in Auchtermuchty. Otherwise use any game stock or, as a last resort, a reduced dark chicken stock.

The elderberry jelly adds a sweetness to the sauce; you could substitute blackcurrant or redcurrant, if you cannot find elderberries. I collect pounds of them from our churchyard in Cramond in September to make jelly, or I mix them with brambles and apples in jams or pies.

The thyme crust for the purée is best when made with good Italian bread, as it is close-textured and absorbs the oil and thyme flavours well. The crunchy topping provides a contrasting texture to the soft purée.

Red cabbage is a classic accompaniment with any game; add some peeled chestnuts, when they are available. If you wish to, garnish the venison with a spoonful of natural yoghurt – its sharpness cuts through the strong game flavour.

The pudding is deliberately light and refreshing after the game. Blaeberries are gathered on the moors in Scotland, from July to September. They make delicious tarts and jellies. If unavailable, blueberries (often sold in large supermarkets) are a good substitute. The dish would be enhanced even more by cooking the berries in a home-made sloe gin instead of the clear spirit.

THE STARTER AND PUDDING CAN BE PREPARED IN ADVANCE (NOT TOO LONG FOR THE AÏOLI) AND REHEATED, IF NECESSARY. THE RED CABBAGE CAN BE COOKED THE DAY BEFORE AND HEATED THROUGH. ONLY THE VENISON AND PURÉE NEED LAST-MINUTE ATTENTION

As to wines to accompany this dinner, I suggest something sharp to balance the pungent aïoli, for example, a Frascati or Verdicchio. Follow this with a gutsy red – a good Bordeaux or Rhône wine, for example – perfect with the venison. And to finish, a sweet wine to balance the citric yoghurt ice: try Moscato d'Asti Naturale.

Tart of Arbroath Smokies with Aïoli

SHORTCRUST PASTRY

250 g (9 oz) plain flour, sifted
4 ml (¾ tsp) salt
150 g (5 oz) unsalted butter, diced
1 egg, medium
15 ml (1 tbsp) olive oil

FILLING

275 g (10 oz) Arbroath smokie 'flesh'
(about 2 smokies; or any other 'hot-smoked' haddock)
3 eggs, medium, beaten
10 ml (2 tsp) lemon juice, freshly squeezed
pinch of cayenne pepper
salt
125–150 ml (4–5 fl oz) double cream

AÏOLI

2 cloves garlic, peeled
1 egg, medium
15 ml (1 tbsp) lemon juice
125–150 ml (4–5 fl oz) sunflower oil
50–75 ml (2–3 fl oz) olive oil

TO FINISH

flat parsley or chervil

1. **To make pastry**: place flour, salt and butter in food processor. Mix briefly, then add egg mixed with olive oil through feeder tube. Wait till dough 'balls' (add a drop or two of extra oil if necessary). Wrap in clingfilm and refrigerate for at least 2 hours.

2. Roll out and line buttered 23 cm (9 inch) flan tin. (You will have a little pastry left; this freezes well.) Prick the base with a fork, then rest pastry in fridge for half an hour. Bake blind in pre-heated oven 200°C (400°F/Gas 6) for 10 minutes with baking beans, then 5 minutes without beans. Remove and cool slightly. Reduce oven to 190°C (375°F/Gas 5).

3. **For filling:** mix together flaked smokies, eggs, lemon juice, cayenne, then stir in cream. Taste for seasoning (if you can bear it!) and add salt if necessary (smokies are naturally salty, so beware). Spoon into part-baked pastry case and bake for about 25–30 minutes till lightly brown and puffed up.

4. **For aïoli:** crush garlic with a little salt. Put into food processor, add egg and process for 30 seconds, then add lemon juice and process for 10 seconds. With machine running, slowly pour in oils through feeder tube until consistency of mayonnaise is reached. Taste and add salt or lemon juice if necessary.

5. Serve wedges of the warm tart with a good spoonful of aïoli, garnished with flat parsley or chervil.

TART FREEZES FOR ABOUT A MONTH. AÏOLI CANNOT BE
FROZEN

Venison with Elderberries

2 venison fillets, each about 325 g (12 oz)
350 ml (12 fl oz) good red wine
450 ml (15 fl oz) venison stock, reduced
30 ml (2 tbsp) elderberry jelly
30 ml (2 tbsp) hazelnut oil
handful of thyme sprigs
15 ml (1 tbsp) olive oil
50 g (2 oz) unsalted butter
salt and freshly milled pepper

TO FINISH

a few elderberries, fresh or frozen (thawed)
thyme sprigs

1. Trim venison, brush with hazelnut oil and press thyme all over. Cover and place in fridge for 2–4 hours.

2. Heat olive oil and 25 g (1 oz) butter in heavy frying pan; brown and seal venison for 2 minutes on each side (maximum 6 minutes). Remove to warm oven 150°C (300°F/Gas 2) for a maximum of 8 minutes.

3. Deglaze pan (dilute concentrated juices) with wine, reduce to half.

4. Add stock, reduce to half. Add thyme and press down with the back of a spoon to extract flavour.

5. Add jelly, stir well and reduce till sauce-like consistency. Lower heat and add knob of butter to give gloss. Season to taste and strain (I prefer using butter muslin, but a fine sieve will do).

6. Cut venison into 1 cm (½ inch) slices and fan around cabbage. Pour sauce around meat and decorate with thyme and elderberries.

Braised Red Cabbage

10 ml (2 tsp) olive oil
15 g (½ oz) butter
50 g (2 oz) unsmoked bacon (rind removed), chopped
1 onion, peeled, chopped
2 cloves garlic, peeled, crushed
450 g (1 lb) red cabbage, sliced
1 cooking apple, peeled, cored, chopped
300 ml (10 fl oz) mixed red wine and stock
pinch of cloves
freshly grated nutmeg
2 ml (¼ tsp) salt
freshly ground pepper

1. Heat oil and butter in large pan and sauté the bacon, onion and garlic until softened. Add red cabbage and cook, stirring, for 10 minutes.

2. Add apple with remaining ingredients and bring to boil.

3. Transfer to ovenproof dish, cover and cook in preheated oven 160°C (325°F/Gas 3) for 2–3 hours.

DO NOT FREEZE CABBAGE OR VENISON

Parsnip and Potato Purée with Thyme Crust

600 g (1¼ lb) parsnips, peeled
325 g (12 oz) potatoes, peeled
nutmeg
40 g (1½ oz) butter
125 ml (4 fl oz) double cream
coarse sea salt
freshly ground pepper

TOPPING

50 g (2 oz) fresh white breadcrumbs
a little olive oil
knob of butter
handful of thyme leaves (pulled off stalks)

1. Cook the parsnips and potatoes in boiling, salted water until just tender; drain. Pass through a mouli-légume, or mash to smooth purée using a potato masher.

2. Gently heat the butter, cream, nutmeg and seasoning in a heavy-based pan. Add vegetables and heat through, stirring.

3. For the topping, fry the breadcrumbs in a little olive oil and butter, with thyme leaves, until crisp. Add more oil, if too dry. Sprinkle over parsnip and potato purée to serve.

DO NOT FREEZE

Lemon Yoghurt Ice
with Blaeberries in Gin

ICE-CREAM

juice of 1 large lemon (preferably unwaxed; otherwise scrub well)
grated rind of lemon
100 g (4 oz) caster sugar
500 ml (16 fl oz) Greek yoghurt

BLAEBERRIES

450 g (1 lb) blaeberries (or blueberries)
60–75 ml (4–5 tbsp) gin
25 g (1 oz) butter
25 g (1 oz) caster sugar

1. **For the ice:** combine the lemon juice, rind, sugar and yoghurt in
   a large bowl. Once well mixed, cover tightly with clingfilm and
   place in freezer, or ice-cream machine.

2. After 1½ hours–2 hours (depending on the efficiency of your
   freezer), remove bowl and beat contents. Return to freezer-proof
   container with lid and freeze for another 2 hours until solid. With
   ice-cream machine, it should be ready after half an hour. Remove
   to fridge to soften 15 minutes before serving.

3. **To cook blaeberries:** place them in a saucepan with the gin, butter
   and sugar, and heat carefully until berries are warmed through
   and glazed (about 10–15 minutes).

4. **To serve:** spoon the blaeberries on to plates, with some of the
   juices, and top with a scoop or quenelle shape of yoghurt ice.
   Serve immediately.

DO NOT FREEZE BLAEBERRIES ONCE COOKED

DAVID WILSON, chef/proprietor of The Peat Inn, Cupar, Fife, since 1972, has been the pioneer of Scotland's emerging *haute cuisine*. The emphasis at The Peat Inn is to reflect the local area by the use of top-quality Scottish produce. This is David Wilson's recipe for a venison dish.

Saddle of Venison on a Base of Forcemeat and Wild Mushrooms

SERVES 6

MEAT

approx. 900 g (2 lb) saddle of venison
(boned and trimmed weight)
a little oil for frying

BASE

75 g (3 oz) venison meat (taken from saddle when trimming)
75 g (3 oz) wild mushrooms (chanterelles or ceps)
15 ml (1 tbsp) double cream
salt and pepper

SAUCE

150 ml (5 fl oz) red wine
15 ml (1 tbsp) sherry vinegar
10 ml (2 tsp) redcurrant jelly
300 ml (10 fl oz) stock, made from bones
50 g (2 oz) butter
salt, pepper

1. **To make base:** finely chop the venison meat and mushrooms in a food processor, then add cream. Mix well and season. (This can be done in advance and reserved.)

2. **To make the sauce:** put red wine, redcurrant jelly and sherry vinegar in saucepan. Reduce until sticky and almost caramelising, then add game stock. Reduce again to required consistency, whisking in butter at the last moment. Check seasoning, keep warm until required.

3. **To cook the saddle:** preheat oven to 230°C (450°C/Gas 8). Seal saddle in a little oil in a sauté pan, then cook in roasting tin in the oven for about 8–10 minutes. Leave to rest in a warm place.

4. **To cook the base:** put a ring mould on a flat baking sheet and spoon in the venison/mushroom farce. Spread this evenly about ½ cm (¼ inch) thick with the back of a spoon then remove ring. Repeat for others. Bake in a hot oven for about 5 minutes until the force-meat sets.

5. **To serve:** put cooked farce on centre of warm plate; cut venison saddle into thin slices and place on top. Surround with the sauce. Serve with fresh, seasoned vegetables.

Chapter Two

I MAKE NO APOLOGIES FOR HAVING A CRAB SOUFFLÉ PRECEDE A PRAWN dish. Scotland's shores have an abundance of fish and shellfish, which I love to use as often as possible. Freshly cooked crabmeat can usually be bought from your fishmonger; he can also advise on cooking times, if you buy crab live. On holiday on Islay, off the west coast of Scotland, we negotiate with local fishermen to buy some of their catch. We boil crabs and eat them simply with fresh brown bread and good mayonnaise. A more elaborate way to use crab is in a soufflé, which is not at all difficult to produce. The combination, both colour and flavour, with nasturtiums, is exquisite. The nasturtium leaves taste peppery and the flowers rather spicy and they combine well in salads, with pasta or seafood. Keep the flowers whole, for optimum visual impact.

The main dish effuses sunshine: the tomatoes, dried in the sun; the basil, which is essentially a summer herb; and the pasta – all are reminiscent of a sun-drenched Italy. Since raw prawns can sometimes be difficult to obtain, a firm white fish like North Sea haddock, cut into chunks, makes a reasonable alternative; alter cooking time according to the thickness of the fillets. Langoustines are even better – many are caught around Scotland's shores. They can be shelled and deveined like prawns, but if you are squeamish, blanch them first, for they must be bought live. Basil cannot withstand frost, so in the winter, it can be kept on the kitchen window, ready to be plucked as needed. It responds better to shredding or tearing with the fingers, rather than chopping with a knife. Dried basil lacks the depth of flavour and perfume of the fresh, so this should only be used as a last resort. A better alternative to dried herbs is to freeze sealed polythene bags of the fresh herbs in the plentiful summer months, and use them in sauces or casseroles straight from the freezer.

After the strong fishy flavours, a fruit sorbet cleanses the palate. And what better than another sunshine fruit – mango – combined

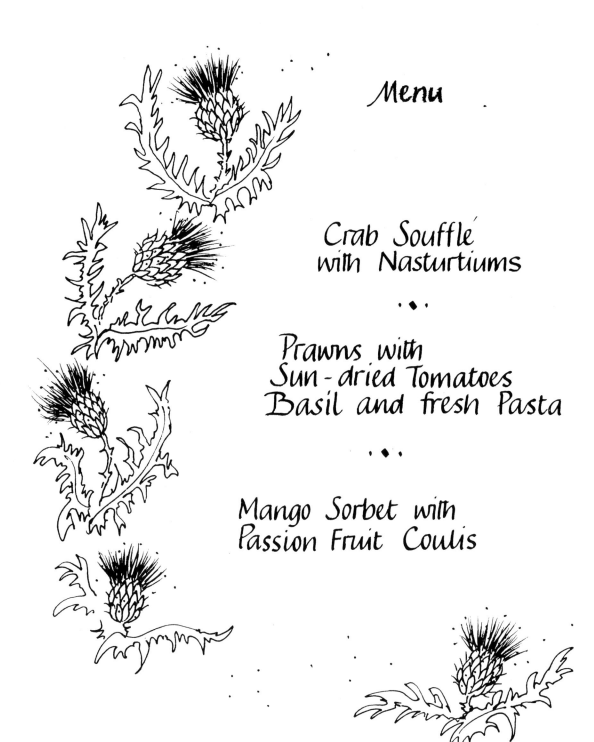

Menu

Crab Soufflé
with Nasturtiums

• •

Prawns with
Sun-dried Tomatoes
Basil and fresh Pasta

• •

Mango Sorbet with
Passion Fruit Coulis

with a sauce of passion-fruits. Do not be put off by passion-fruits' deeply wrinkled skin – inside is an aromatic sweet pulp. Mangoes are also sweet, fragrant and exotic. Their combination transports your tastebuds to warmth and sunshine. You could come back down to earth by offering homely Scottish shortbread biscuits to accompany.

ONLY THE SALAD DRESSING, THE PASTA, THE SORBET AND THE COULIS CAN BE PREPARED IN ADVANCE. THE SOUFFLÉS CAN BE PREPARED UP UNTIL THE END OF STAGE 3, BUT THE PRAWNS MUST BE COOKED AT THE LAST MINUTE

The perfume of nasturtium flowers can be enhanced by a fragrant white wine, such as a top-quality German Riesling. The prawns or langoustines can be eaten with the same wine, or an Australian Chardonnay, which is the perfect partner for shellfish. The pudding does not lend itself to wine, as the natural sweetness of the tropical fruits would be overcome by a sweet dessert wine.

Crab Soufflé with Nasturtiums

INDIVIDUAL CRAB SOUFFLÉS

175 g (6 oz) crabmeat (more white meat to brown meat)
25 g (1 oz) butter
25 g (1 oz) plain flour
250 ml (9 fl oz) milk
4 eggs, small
good pinch cayenne pepper
salt, freshly ground pepper
25 g (1 oz) grated Parmesan cheese

1. Melt butter in saucepan, stir in flour to make roux. Gradually beat in milk, whisk until thickened and coming to the boil. Remove from heat, season with salt, pepper and cayenne, and cool for 10 minutes.

2. Separate eggs, and beat yolks into mixture, one at a time. Add the crabmeat and stir well. Check seasoning.

3. At this stage, you can prepare up to 2 hours in advance by pressing clingfilm on to surface and setting aside. Keep cool, but not too cold. Bring back to room temperature before next stage.

4. Butter 4 ramekins – 8 cm (3 inches) – very well, and sprinkle Parmesan all round sides and base. The mixture will in fact be slightly too much for 4 ramekins, but to make less is not worthwhile. Cover any left-overs and cook next day; results will not be as splendid, but still very tasty.

5. Whisk egg whites till stiff; fold gently into crab mixture (having 'loosened' it by folding in only one tablespoon at first, then gradually the rest, with a metal spoon).

6. Spoon mixture carefully into ramekins, up to the rim. Keep it level, don't heap it over the top.

7. Bake in centre of preheated oven 190°C (375°F/Gas 5) for 25–30 minutes, till well risen and brown on top.

8. Serve at once with nasturtium salad. Either place ramekin on plate, with side serving of salad; or, even better, wait for one minute, then pass a knife around the edge of the ramekin, and invert on to the palm of your hand. Quickly invert it back on to the plate, so it is right way up. Pile some salad all around and serve immediately. (You may want to bake an extra soufflé with remaining mixture, just in case you have problems inverting all 4 perfectly!)

NASTURTIUM SALAD

selection of lamb's lettuce and oakleaf lettuce, washed, dried
large handful of nasturtium leaves and flowers
(wash carefully only if necessary)
15 ml (1 tbsp) balsamic vinegar
75 ml (3 tbsp) sunflower oil
15 ml (1 tbsp) hazelnut oil
2 ml (½ tsp) Dijon mustard
salt, freshly ground black pepper

1. Combine all salad leaves and flowers in a bowl.

2. Mix vinegar with mustard and seasoning in another bowl, then whisk in oils to form emulsion. (The delicate nature of edible flowers means you should be sparing with vinegar and avoid heavy oils; use olive oil only if it is a light one.)

3. Reserve a couple of flowers to decorate, then pour over as much dressing as needed, toss and serve.

NONE OF THE STARTER CAN BE FROZEN

Prawns with Sun-dried Tomatoes, Basil and Fresh Pasta

PRAWNS WITH SUN-DRIED TOMATOES AND BASIL

30 ml (2 tbsp) sun-dried tomatoes in oil, drained, slivered
30 ml (2 tbsp) oil from the tomatoes
2 cloves garlic, peeled, crushed
700 g (1 ½ lb) raw prawns (each weighing about 25 g (1 oz),
or langoustines
50 g (2 oz) shallots, peeled, chopped finely
5–6 large leaves fresh basil
freshly ground pepper
150 ml (5 fl oz) light chicken (or fish) stock
75 ml (3 fl oz) dry white wine (or Vermouth)
150 ml (5 fl oz) double cream
25 g (1 oz) freshly grated Parmesan

TO FINISH

few small sprigs fresh basil, to garnish

1. Shell the prawns, but keep the tail intact. Carefully remove the black thread which runs down the back (simply pull it out slowly). Blanch and shell langoustines and cook according to size (usually less time than prawns, which are not blanched). Wash prawns or langoustines and pat dry well.

2. Heat oil in heavy pan, add garlic and shallots and cook for a minute, or until just softened. Add prawns or langoustines and cook for no more than 1 minute each side, until opaque.

3. Remove prawns or langoustines, set aside.

4. Add stock, tomatoes, wine, cream, a good grinding of pepper and the basil leaves, torn or shredded roughly. Bring to the boil, then lower heat and reduce to half; then add Parmesan and stir through. Add prawns or langoustines and warm through for 20 seconds or so.

5. Serve prawns with sauce on a twirl of basil-flavoured pasta, and garnish with a sprig of fresh basil.

BASIL PASTA

225 g (8 oz) strong white flour
4 ml (¾ tsp) salt
1 egg, large
1 egg yolk (reserve white)
small handful basil leaves
5 ml (1 tsp) dry white wine (optional)
5 ml (1 tsp) olive oil

1. Put flour, salt and basil in food processor, and process for a few seconds. Add wine, oil, egg and egg yolk, and process briefly until dough begins to hold together (or 'balls'). Add reserved egg white if necessary to bind.

2. Wrap in clingfilm and leave to rest in fridge for 30 minutes.

3. Put dough through a pasta machine until thin and silky, then cut into tagliatelle. (I roll the pasta out to the penultimate setting.) Without a machine, simply roll out the dough as thinly as possible and cut into strips.

INDIVIDUAL ARBROATH SMOKIE TART WITH AÏOLI

LANGOUSTINES WITH SUN-DRIED TOMATOES, BASIL AND
FRESH PASTA

4. At this stage you can either hang the pasta over a broom or the back of a chair to dry (in which case cook for longer than if just made), or cook immediately.

5. Cook tagliatelle in boiling salted water (to which you have added a little oil, so it does not stick) for about 30 seconds. (If it has dried a little, cook for 2–3 minutes.)

6. Drain well and serve with prawns.

PASTA CAN BE FROZEN, AND COOKED WITHOUT THAWING
FOR 3–4 MINUTES

Mango Sorbet with Passion-fruit Coulis

SORBET

3 large ripe mangoes (unbruised)
juice of 1 lime
100g (4 oz) caster sugar
60 ml (4 tbsp) liquid glucose

COULIS

4 passion-fruit
15 g (½ oz) caster sugar
juice of ½ lime (or lemon)

TO FINISH

juliennes of lime zest, blanched for 1 minute, then refreshed and dried
slivers of fresh mango

1. **For sorbet:** wash and dry mangoes. Skin them, remove flesh (there should be about 500 g (1 lb 2 oz)) and place in food processor with lime juice and sugar.

2. Heat glucose (either in the top of a double boiler, or on medium in microwave for 2–3 minutes) until melted. Quickly whisk into mango purée, then strain through fine sieve.

3. Freeze in an ice-cream machine until well churned (mine takes about 25 minutes). Without a machine, place in freezer on 'fast-freeze', and remove to whisk every 30 minutes till solid.

4. **For coulis:** halve the passion-fruit, scoop out the pulp and seeds into a food processor. Add the lime juice and sugar, and work to a purée. Pass through a sieve. (Taste to check for sweetness; add more, if required.)

5. **To serve:** remove sorbet to room temperature a short time before ready to eat. Place a couple of small spoonfuls on plate and pour a little coulis alongside. Garnish with some pared, blanched lime zest, or some slivers of fresh mango. Buttery shortbread (see page 114) makes a nice crunchy accompaniment.

FREEZE SORBET; DO NOT FREEZE COULIS.

NICK NAIRN is chef/proprietor of Braeval Old Mill, near Aberfoyle. He is an enthusiastic young chef, who has built up a reputation for innovative dishes made with the freshest of Scottish ingredients. Pasta is one of his passions, so here is one of his seafood and pasta combinations.

Photograph © *The Scotsman*

Lasagne of Brill, Squat Lobsters and Mussels with a Herb Velouté

SERVES 4

LASAGNE

1400 g (3 lb) brill, filleted and cut into 40 g (1½ oz) pieces
20 squat lobsters, blanched, shelled; reserve best 4 for garnish
450 g (1 lb) mussels, scrubbed, debearded, steamed, shelled;
reserve juices
24 large spinach leaves, blanched, refreshed, squeezed dry, tossed
in seasoned butter
1 large carrot, peeled, cut in fine long julienne strips, cooked
lightly in butter
12 x 10 cm (4 inch) diameter circles of cooked pasta (pasta made
with 275 g (10 oz) flour, 2 eggs, 3 yolks, 3 ml (½ tsp) salt; rolled to
thinnest setting and cut into circles. See page 31
for further instructions.)
15 ml (1 tbsp) of (mixed) chives, tarragon, chervil, coriander; all
chopped
225 ml (8 fl oz) velouté (see below)
125 ml (4 fl oz) fish stock
125 ml (4 fl oz) mussel juice
squeeze of lemon juice

VELOUTÉ

5 shallots, very finely chopped
15 g (½ oz) butter
300 ml (10 fl oz) Noilly Prat
300 ml (10 fl oz) fish stock
300 ml (10 fl oz) double cream
salt, freshly ground pepper

1. **For velouté:** sweat shallots in butter until soft, add Noilly Prat, and reduce until syrupy; add fish stock and repeat; add cream, and simmer gently until thickened. Pass through a fine mesh sieve and reserve the cream velouté.

2. **For pasta:** cook circles for 2 minutes in boiling salted water, drain, refresh, then pat dry. Lay them out on a lightly oiled tray and cover with lightly oiled clingfilm.

3. Heat through velouté, stock and mussel juice in large flat pan. Season to taste with salt, pepper, lemon juice.

4. Heat spinach through in the seasoned butter. Add brill to velouté and cook gently for 45–60 seconds.

5. Reheat pasta circles in simmering water.

6. Add squat lobsters and mussels to brill, and heat for a further 30 seconds (do not boil).

7. **To finish:** check fish is cooked, check seasoning. In warmed shallow soup bowls, layer spinach, pasta and fish. Finish with some spinach on a pasta circle, place a nest of carrot juliennes, then reserved squat lobster on top. Blend cooking liquid with hand blender until frothy, add the chopped herbs, then spoon over the lasagne and serve.

As wine to accompany this dish, Nick Nairn recommends a good Mersault or Australian Chardonnay.

Chapter Three

THE FLAVOURS ARE ROBUST AND THE SEASON DECIDEDLY AUTUMNAL. This is a menu for those with hearty appetites, yet discerning palates, for here many interesting tastes come together.

The starter is unusual because of the pasta dough. A friend, who cannot take any wheat products, asked me to find a suitable pasta recipe. Using all chestnut flour (available from good Italian delicatessens) results in an acceptable, if rather heavy dough. My definitive recipe, however, incorporates chestnut and wheat flour, and is light, nutty and delicious. It is the perfect vehicle for the Christmas flavours of turkey and cranberries. Late autumn is an ideal time for this menu, therefore, with the start of festive fare in the shops, and before the fresh brambles disappear.

The beef dish is delightfully succulent. It incorporates the strong flavour of olives in a savoury stuffing. The bread, flavoured with roasted fennel seeds and a few more black olives, is a satisfying way to mop up juices from the meat and the sauce. The salad dressing is unusual as it contains horseradish relish – which should be tasted carefully, as different jars contain varying strengths of relish. Rocket is a great favourite of mine. It can survive outside, even in Scotland, for most of the winter. Its rather nutty flavour lends itself to hazelnut oil-based dressings, for a change from the horseradish one. It is also used to make a rather pungent sauce, which I discovered in Tuscany. Although the basic components differ, it is similar to pesto in its uses.

The pudding is a harmonious marriage of tastes. Brambles go perfectly with lemon curd, as they do with oats and with apples. Frozen fruit will do very well, but reduce the amount of juice to cook with it. The combination of a hot pudding and a refreshing cold ice is nectar. The ice-cream should be made only with home-made lemon curd; the cloying, bright yellow contents of some supermarket jars bear no resemblance to the real thing. It is also an ice-cream which stands well on its own, decorated with lemon slivers or mint.

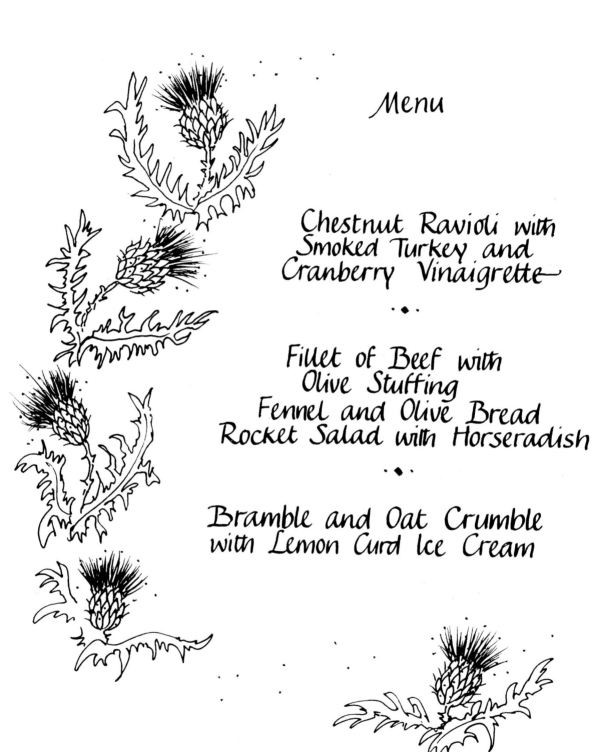

Menu

Chestnut Ravioli with
Smoked Turkey and
Cranberry Vinaigrette

• ◆ •

Fillet of Beef with
Olive Stuffing
Fennel and Olive Bread
Rocket Salad with Horseradish

• ◆ •

Bramble and Oat Crumble
with Lemon Curd Ice Cream

THE RAVIOLI PASTA CAN BE PREPARED IN ADVANCE AND
REFRIGERATED. THE COMPLETED RAVIOLI ARE BETTER
EITHER JUST MADE OR FROZEN. THE BEEF CAN BE PREPARED
UP TO THE END OF STAGE 2 AND KEPT IN THE FRIDGE OVER-
NIGHT. THE BREAD AND PUDDING ARE BEST MADE ON THE
DAY, AND THE SALAD MUST BE DONE AT THE LAST MINUTE

The bold flavour of a Barolo wine matches the earthiness of the
starter. The beef would fare well with a lively young Chianti or
Valpolicella. For the pudding, a glass of Muscat de Beaumes de
Venise or Moscato di Pantelleria would make this hot, fruity
crumble heavenly.

Chestnut Ravioli with Smoked Turkey and Cranberry Vinaigrette

CHESTNUT RAVIOLI

175 g (6 oz) strong white flour
50 g (2 oz) chestnut flour
1 large egg
1 egg yolk
2 ml (½ tsp) salt

FILLING

50 g (2 oz) ricotta cheese (cream cheese will do if ricotta unavailable)
50 g (2 oz) smoked turkey (Pastrami is a good alternative)
½ onion, finely chopped
1 clove garlic, peeled, crushed
8 ml (½ tbsp) olive oil
salt, freshly ground pepper

CRANBERRY VINAIGRETTE

15 ml (1 tbsp) balsamic vinegar
30 ml (2 tbsp) good cranberry sauce
45 ml (3 tbsp) sunflower oil
30 ml (2 tbsp) olive oil
sea salt, freshly ground pepper

TO FINISH

25–50g (1-2 oz) unsalted butter, melted
(cranberries, blanched until skins nearly bursting)

1. **To make filling:** heat oil in pan, soften garlic and onion for a couple of minutes. Add chopped turkey and ricotta and season. Set aside.

2. **To make ravioli:** make pasta as described in Chapter 2. Roll out to penultimate setting (or as thinly as possible, if rolling by hand). Using a 5 cm (2 inch) cutter (or whichever size you like, simply adjust cooking times), stamp out circles of the dough and place 5 ml (1 tsp) of the filling on the centre of the circles. Dampen edges, then either fold the circle over to make a half-moon shape, or top with another circle and trim edges with fluted pastry cutter. Sprinkle with flour and leave to dry on floured wire rack.

3. **To make cranberry dressing:** mix vinegar with salt and pepper, then whisk in cranberry sauce and sufficient oils to make thick, but pouring consistency.

4. **To cook ravioli:** bring a large pan of salted water to the boil, adding a dash of oil, then slide in ravioli carefully, and cook until just done (about 3–4 minutes).

5. **To serve:** drain ravioli and quickly pat off excess water with kitchen roll. Place 2 or 3 (depending on size) on individual warmed plates, pour over a little melted butter, then drizzle over some of the cranberry dressing. If you feel it needs extra garnish, some blanched fresh cranberries look good.

RAVIOLI CAN BE FROZEN; COOK FROM FROZEN FOR 5–6 MINUTES. DO NOT FREEZE DRESSING

Fillet of Beef with Olive Stuffing

MEAT

1 whole piece fillet of beef (550 g (1 ¼ lb) trimmed weight)
30 ml (2 tbsp) olive oil
15 ml (1 tbsp) cognac
salt, freshly ground pepper

STUFFING

50 g (2 oz) unsmoked streaky bacon (rind removed),
finely chopped
10 ml (2 tsp) fresh rosemary leaves, chopped
25 g (1 oz) fresh white breadcrumbs (a bread roll weighs about
25 g (1 oz), so I often use this, outer crust and all. For a finer
texture, remove crusts.)
12 black olives, pitted, finely chopped
1 clove garlic, peeled, crushed
1 shallot, finely chopped
30 ml (2 tbsp) olive oil
freshly ground pepper

SAUCE

225 ml (8 fl oz) beef stock (*Fonds de Cuisine* will do, if home-made
not available)
1 clove garlic, peeled, but left whole
5 ml (1 tsp) horseradish relish
15 ml (1 tbsp) red wine vinegar
175 ml (6 fl oz) red wine (full-bodied)
salt, pepper

1. **To prepare stuffing:** heat 15 ml (1 tbsp) oil in pan, add garlic, shallots, bacon. Cook for 2–3 minutes till soft and golden, then add other ingredients. Stir well and remove from heat. Add

remaining 15 ml (1 tbsp) oil to bind, pepper to taste, and leave to cool.

2. **For meat:** trim fillet of any membrane and fat. With sharp knife, cut through length of fillet to open up into rectangle. Season then place filling down middle, roll up meat around it and tie securely with butchers' string (your butcher should be able to supply this). Don't worry if some stuffing comes out – just poke it back! Leave in cool place.

3. **To cook meat:** if it has been refrigerated, bring back to room temperature. Then, using a pastry brush, 'paint' all over the meat with 15 ml (1 tbsp) oil mixed with the cognac. Lightly season meat. Preheat the oven to 230°C (450°F/Gas 8), allowing up to half an hour to reach this high temperature.

4. Heat remaining oil in heavy pan or roasting tin till very hot, add meat and seal all over (this takes about 4 minutes). Place in the preheated oven 230°C (450°F/Gas 8) for 18 minutes. (The result will be medium-rare; for rare, 15 minutes; for medium, 21 minutes.)

5. Remove to warm dish and wrap tightly in double foil. Retain any meat juices. Rest for 15 minutes before slicing into 1 cm (½ inch) slices with a very sharp knife.

6. **For sauce:** place wine in pan with garlic and vinegar. Bring to the boil, then reduce to one third. Add stock, reduce to half. Add horseradish relish, taste for seasoning, then strain through muslin. Add any reserved meat juices to sauce and serve around slices of beef.

7. The stuffing is rather crumbly; if you prefer a more solid texture to produce thin slices, bind the stuffing ingredients with a little beaten egg before filling beef and cooking.

Fennel and Olive Bread

225 g (8 oz) strong white flour
(or Italian wheat-type OO flour)
pinch of sugar
25 g (1 oz) black olives, pitted, chopped, patted dry on kitchen
paper
8 ml (½ tbsp) fennel seeds, roasted (this extracts maximum
flavour)
2 ml (½ tsp) salt
15 g (½ oz) fresh yeast. If using dried yeast, follow instructions on
packet
15 ml (1 tbsp) olive oil
150–175 ml (5–6 fl oz) lukewarm water
(olive oil, to finish)

1. Dissolve yeast in a little of the water, with a pinch of sugar. Leave for about 10 minutes, until frothy.

2. Sift the flour and salt into bowl, pour on yeast mixture and add oil, fennel and olives. Add sufficient lukewarm water to bind to a soft dough. Knead for about 10 minutes until smooth, then roll in a little oil, and leave to rise in a warm place, covered. (I put bread doughs in my airing cupboard to rise; it takes at least an hour to double in volume.)

3. Knock back the dough, knead briefly then shape into an oval and place on an oiled baking sheet. (The dough should be about 1 cm (½ inch) thick.) Press your knuckles all over dough to make little dimples, then pour some oil all over, to coat. (It will run into the dimples, making the bread even more moist.)

4. Let the bread rise again for 30 minutes then bake in a preheated oven 230°C (450°F/Gas 8) for about 20 minutes until puffed up and golden.

Rocket Salad with Horseradish

1 large bunch watercress, washed
1 large bunch rocket, trimmed
25 ml (1 fl oz) sherry vinegar
100 ml (4 fl oz) extra virgin olive oil
salt, freshly ground pepper
7 ml (1 ½ tsp) horseradish relish (not sauce)
2 ml (½ tsp) Dijon mustard

1. Place watercress and rocket in salad bowl.

2. Combine all remaining ingredients by shaking them together in screw-top jar (or whizz in food processor). Pour some of this dressing over salad leaves, toss and serve.

BEEF AND SALAD CANNOT BE FROZEN. BREAD CAN BE FROZEN; THAW FOR AN HOUR THEN RE-WARM IN OVEN.

Bramble and Oat Crumble with Lemon Curd Ice-cream

FILLING

450 g (1 lb) brambles (blackberries)
225 g (8 oz) cooking apples, peeled, chopped finely
15 ml (1 tbsp) apple juice
75 g (3 oz) caster sugar

TOPPING

25 g (1 oz) hazelnuts, toasted, chopped
50 g (2 oz) plain wholemeal flour
75 g (3 oz) porridge oats
50 g (2 oz) light muscovado sugar
1 ml (¼ tsp) ground mace
50 g (2 oz) unsalted butter
45–60 ml (3–4 tbsp) sunflower oil

1. Place fruit in buttered ovenproof dish, sprinkle with sugar and apple juice.

2. Make topping by rubbing butter roughly into flour, then add sugar, hazelnuts, oats and mace. Add sufficient oil to combine to crumble mixture.

3. Spread evenly over fruit and bake in preheated oven 180°C (350°F/Gas 4) for 45 minutes. Serve warm, not hot, with a spoonful (or two) of the ice-cream.

LEMON CURD ICE-CREAM

The rind of 3 large lemons
225 g (8 oz) sugar
125 g (4 oz) unsalted butter
3 eggs
175 ml (6 fl oz) lemon juice
500 ml (16 fl oz) natural yoghurt (not the set variety)

1. **To make lemon curd:** sieve the eggs, then beat lightly. Mix in the lemon rind and the freshly squeezed juice, the butter in pieces, and the sugar. Place in the top of a double-boiler or in a bowl over a pan of simmering water. Heat gently, stirring constantly, until sugar dissolves and mixture thickens (about 20 minutes). Cool, then use as required.

2. Slowly stir 325 g (12 oz) lemon curd into the yoghurt until well mixed. Pour into a freezerproof container and freeze until firm. (This takes between 3 and 4 hours, depending on your freezer. For speedier results, freeze in individual ramekins.)

DO NOT FREEZE BRAMBLE CRUMBLE

BRUCE SANGSTER, chef at Murrayshall Country House Hotel, Scone, near Perth, is a firm believer in the use of top-quality Scottish produce, within its season. Beef is one of his favourites. Here he shares one of his recipes.

Medallion of Scotch Beef
with a bone marrow, herb and horseradish crust, served with caramelised shallots and a Guinness Sauce

SERVES 4

4 x 150 g (5 oz) medallions of Scotch beef fillet
50 g (2 oz) bone marrow
fresh thyme, chives, parsley, finely chopped
100g (4 oz) brioche or breadcrumbs, browned
25 g (1 oz) grated fresh horseradish
20 small shallots, peeled
pinch of caster sugar
25 g (1 oz) onion, finely chopped
25 g (1 oz) carrot, finely chopped
25 g (1 oz) celery, finely chopped
1 bay leaf
150 ml (5 fl oz) red wine
300 ml (10 fl oz) good jellied beef stock
1 small bottle Guinness
50 g (2 oz) cold butter
assorted herbs, for garnish
selection of baby carrots, turnips, courgette, mangetout, haricots verts, broccoli, cauliflower

1. Roughly chop the marrow and lightly mix in the chopped herbs, crumbs and horseradish.

2. Brown the shallots in a little oil, add the sugar, caramelise and add a little water. Cook in a hot oven, until golden brown.

3. Blanch all vegetables in boiling water.

4. Seal the beef in a little oil in a hot pan and cook for 4 minutes; do not overcook. Then remove and store in a warm place.

5. Add the diced vegetables to the cooking pan and brown quickly. Deglaze with red wine and reduce. Add the Guinness and reduce, then add the beef jelly.

6. Cook rapidly for 6–7 minutes until reduced; pass through a muslin.

7. Crown the beef with the crumb mixture and flash through a hot oven until the crust is brown.

8. Reheat the vegetables.

9. Place the shallots in the centre of 4 hot plates. Surround with the hot vegetables. Then place the beef on to the shallots.

10. Finish the sauce with knobs of butter and seasoning, then spoon around the beef. Decorate with herbs.

BRAMBLE AND OAT CRUMBLE WITH LEMON CURD ICE-CREAM

PARSNIP AND CRAB SOUP

Chapter Four

THERE IS A BLEND OF THE OLD WITH THE NEW IN THIS MENU. THE USE of olive oil to garnish soup is new to many, but parsnip soup is an old favourite. Crab makes an ideal partner to the root vegetable; the depth of flavours is wonderful and enhanced by the fruitiest olive oil drizzled over at the end.

Stovies are an old-fashioned Scottish dish which was part of my childhood. My parents are from Dundee, and they used to eat them regularly, either as a complete dish or with sausages. Special dripping would be bought from the butcher's for the occasion, for Dundee people had roast meat very seldom. The perfect recipe uses dripping from a roast, which has a set layer of meat juices underneath. Since stovies are, in this menu, merely a side dish to partridge – which many connoisseurs consider to be the best game bird of all – appetites may have to be forcibly restrained, for they are very 'more-ish'. The new element in the main course is a Chinese-style influence in the stir-fried cabbage; its crunchy texture is retained by using this cooking method. Gone is the limp over-cooked vegetable reminiscent of school lunches.

What is more old-fashioned than apple pie? Everyone's grand-mother makes the best! I have mixed the apples with mincemeat, for a change. I make jars of mincemeat each October, hoping they will last two Christmases; somehow they never do. The new element is the quince ice-cream, which is quite exquisite. The intense flavour comes from quince eau-de-vie. Quinces are very hard and dense, so take a long time to cook, but it is worth waiting. The eau-de-vie has the full fragrance and scent of the fruit which are, sadly, rather scarce in Scotland. Japonica is more common and its fruit makes an acceptable substitute for quince jelly. If you can obtain any fresh quinces, substitute the apples in the pie with one, sliced as thinly as possible.

Menu

Parsnip and Crab Soup
with Olive Oil

•••

Partridge with Red Wine Sauce
Stovies
Stir-fried Cabbage with Garlic

•••

Apple and Mincemeat Pie
with Quince Ice Cream

THE PARSNIP SOUP CAN BE PREPARED TO THE PURÉEING
STAGE. NONE OF THE MAIN COURSE CAN BE MADE IN
ADVANCE; THE PIE CAN BE READY, UNBAKED, IN THE FRIDGE
OR FREEZER AND COOKED AS REQUIRED

Crab and sherry have a natural affinity and so a chilled fino or dry
amontillado sherry would be perfect to start with. The best red
wine you could afford – French or New World – would complement
partridge, the connoisseur's game bird. The apple and quince
flavours would be enhanced by a sweet German or Austrian wine.

Parsnip and Crab Soup
with Olive Oil

600 ml (20 fl oz) light chicken stock
1 onion, peeled, chopped
1 medium potato, peeled, chopped
2 cloves garlic, peeled, chopped
15 ml (1 tbsp) olive oil
25 g (1 oz) butter
900 g (2 lb) parsnips, peeled, chopped
small glass fino sherry
salt, freshly ground pepper
225 g (8 oz) fresh crabmeat
extra virgin olive oil

1. Soften onion, garlic and potato in oil and butter; add parsnips and cook for 5 minutes.

2. Add stock, bring to boil and simmer (covered) for 30 minutes, until vegetables are tender.

3. Purée in batches, in blender or food processor.

4. Return to saucepan and reheat gently. Add sherry and stir well. Reheat.

5. Check for seasoning and ladle into *warmed* soup bowls.

6. Spoon some crabmeat into middle of each (it will warm through with the heat of the soup and the bowls), and drizzle a little olive oil over each. Serve immediately.

SOUP CAN BE FROZEN UP TO END OF STAGE 3

Partridge with Red Wine Sauce

PARTRIDGE
4 young partridge (oven ready) about 325 g (12 oz) each
4 sprigs thyme
15 ml (1 tbsp) olive oil
50 g (2 oz) unsalted butter
4 rashers unsmoked streaky bacon
salt, pepper

SAUCE
175 ml (6 fl oz) best quality red wine (use the one you will drink
with the dish)
225 ml (8 fl oz) game stock (preferably partridge or pheasant;
otherwise turkey or dark chicken stock will do)
5 ml (1 tsp) redcurrant jelly
10 ml (2 tsp) redcurrant or raspberry vinegar
15 g (½ oz) unsalted butter, cubed
salt, pepper
(thyme, to garnish)

1. **For sauce:** put wine, jelly and vinegar into saucepan. Bring to the boil, lower heat then reduce liquid by two-thirds. Add stock, bring to the boil, then reduce to half. Check seasoning, whisk in butter at last moment. Keep warm.

2. **For birds:** heat oil and butter in roasting pan on top of stove. Brown birds all over (watch your fingers; the fat should be very hot). This takes about 5 minutes. Season well and tuck a bacon roll round a thyme sprig inside each bird.

3. Keep birds in the roasting pan, and cook, breast-side down, in preheated oven 220°C (425°F/Gas 7) for about 20 minutes, depending how pink you like your bird. Baste at least twice with the fat.

4. Turn off the oven, leave the door open while the partridge rest for 10 minutes.

5. Serve them on individual plates, in a 'nest' of cabbage, with the red wine sauce. Garnish with a sprig of thyme.

Stovies

700 g (1 ½ lb) potatoes
275 g (10 oz) onions, peeled, sliced finely into rings
50 g (2 oz) dripping from roast (or butter)
15–30 ml (1–2 tbsp) meat jelly from under roasting fat (or stock)
salt, pepper
(chopped chives or chervil, to garnish)

1. Melt dripping in heavy pan, add onions when hot. Cook gently for about 5 minutes, while peeling potatoes and slicing into 1 cm (½ inch) pieces.

2. Add to pan, stir well, making sure each slice is covered by fat.

3. Add meat jelly or stock, season well, stir carefully and cover with lid. Cook on low heat for 30–35 minutes till potatoes are tender. Shake the pan often, so it does not stick. (The caramelised onions are delicious, however.) Stir only if your pan is not reliable.

4. Serve with a garnish of chopped chives or chervil.

Stir-Fried Cabbage with Garlic

400 g (14 oz) white cabbage
2 large cloves garlic, peeled, crushed
30 ml (2 tbsp) olive oil
salt, freshly ground pepper

1. Heat oil in a very large pan or wok. Add garlic and cook for 1 minute.

2. Slice cabbage as finely as possible, then add and stir-fry for 8–10 minutes. Season well and serve. (If you do not like crunching through garlic, remove with a slotted spoon before adding cabbage; the oil will still be garlic flavoured.)

NONE OF THE MAIN COURSE CAN BE FROZEN

Apple and Mincemeat Pie
with Quince Ice-cream

PASTRY

225 g (8 oz) plain flour, sifted
150 g (5 oz) unsalted butter
15 ml (1 tbsp) caster sugar
1 egg yolk
15–30 ml (1–2 tbsp) water

FILLING

2 cooking apples, large
325 g (12 oz) jar of best mincemeat
30 ml (2 tbsp) brandy
25 g (1 oz) blanched almonds, roughly chopped (optional)

QUINCE ICE-CREAM

250 g (9 oz) fresh Mascarpone cheese
150 g (5 oz) caster sugar
250 ml (9 fl oz) milk
300 ml (10 fl oz) double or whipping cream, whipped
(not too stiff)
30–45 ml (2–3 tbsp) quince eau-de-vie

TO FINISH

Milk, to glaze
Caster sugar, to glaze

1. **For ice-cream:** In a food processor, blend the sugar and the
   Mascarpone together. Heat the milk for 30 seconds, till barely
   warm, then strain into the processor, to combine with the cheese
   (do this with the machine running). Add the eau-de-vie and
   process until mixed. Fold in the cream then pour into an ice-
   cream machine. (If you have no machine, partly freeze then beat

well and return to freezer.) With the alcohol in this ice-cream, it remains quite soft, so should only be removed from the freezer 10 minutes before serving.

2. **To make pastry:** place flour, butter and sugar in food processor and combine to breadcrumb stage. Add egg yolk and sufficient water to 'ball'. Cover with clingfilm and chill for 30 minutes. Roll out two-thirds of pastry to line a 23 cm (9 inch) flan or pie dish. Peel and finely chop apples, mix with other ingredients and pile into pastry case. Roll out remaining pastry and, having dampened edges, place on top, sealing the edges well, and decorating with any left-over pastry if you feel artistic. With a knife make a hole in the centre, brush all over with milk, sprinkle with caster sugar and bake in a preheated oven 200°C (400°F/Gas 6) for about 40 minutes, until golden. (If you have used quince, check it is cooked.)

3. Serve warm with a good dollop of the ice-cream.

FREEZE THE PIE EITHER UNBAKED OR BAKED. IF UNBAKED, THAW FOR ABOUT AN HOUR THEN BAKE AS ABOVE

STEWART CAMERON has been executive chef at the Turnberry Hotel, Ayrshire, since 1980. Classically trained, yet ever keen to incorporate new styles of cooking, he has been instrumental in the gradual development of a new, lighter approach to Scottish cuisine. Partridge is one of his favourite game birds.

Roast Partridge
with Marinated Grapes and Sauternes Essence

SERVES 4

BIRDS

4 young partridge
4 croûtons
4 slices cured pork fat
600 ml (20 fl oz) game stock
450 g (1 lb) grapes (seedless, peeled and marinated)
150 ml (5 fl oz) Sauternes
seasoning
parsley, to garnish
100 g (4 oz) butter

STUFFING

100 g (4 oz) partridge and chicken livers
50 g (2 oz) bacon
25 g (1 oz) onions, chopped
25 g (1 oz) butter
seasoning
50 g (2 oz) grapes
1 sprig thyme

1. **For stuffing:** cut bacon into small pieces and fry gently in butter. Add herbs. Add onions and cook until golden brown.

2. Add chicken and partridge livers, fry quickly and season. Pass through a fine sieve, then place in a basin ready for use.

3. Prepare partridge to oven-ready stage and carefully fill breast cavity with stuffing.

4. Season birds, wrap breast with pork fat and lightly tie.

5. Carefully seal them in a pan and cook in a preheated oven 190°C (375°F/Gas 5).

6. Remove from oven when almost ready. Remove string and pork fat. Drain excess fat from pan carefully, so as not to drain off flavour.

7. Deglaze (dilute) pan with Sauternes. Add game stock and some of grapes; reduce this by half.

8. Pass this sauce all through a fine chinois (sieve).

9. Finish cooking birds in oven, remove and place on to sautéed croûtons.

10. Serve in a dish with remainder of grapes sautéed in butter, sprinkled on top.

11. Add knob of butter to sauce, whisk well and serve separately.

Menu

Aubergine & Goat's Cheese Layer

• • •

Barley & Wild Mushroom Ragout
Leeks in Warm Vinaigrette

• • •

Blackcurrant Pizza with Mascarpone

Chapter Five

THIS VEGETARIAN MENU IS A BLEND OF INDIGENOUS SCOTTISH produce with fairly recent arrivals to the market. The starter is piled high on the plate, rather like a vegetable club sandwich. The aubergine is hot, so it melts the goat's cheese, which is topped by roasted peppers, rocket and pesto sauce. A good olive oil vinaigrette ensures a succulent finish to this dish. A polenta croûton forms the top layer – it is not essential, but adds an interesting crunch to the other textures. Make the polenta according to packet instructions (4 parts water to 1 part polenta is best) and pour on to a flat board to cool. Cut into rounds or slices and paint with olive oil. Grill or fry until crispy – about 5 to 10 minutes – then place on the aubergine layer. If you wanted to serve this as a main dish, you could accompany it with crusty Italian bread.

Back to Scottish basics, barley is one of the stalwarts. Although primarily used in broths and bread – beremeal (barley flour) bannocks are regularly eaten in Orkney – my recipe is for a ragout, or stew, of pearl barley with mushrooms. Since chanterelles and ceps can be found wild in the Scottish countryside, I have suggested you use them. If they are out of season, substitute cultivated shiitake or oyster, or use more dried. I have stipulated the use of dried morels, as their intense flavour adds an earthy dimension. Sadly, they are punitively expensive, but a little goes a long way. A perfect accompaniment to the ragout is leeks, which are steamed lightly and tossed in a fruity vinaigrette while still warm.

The pudding looks like pure gimmickry, but it is, in fact, based on recipes for a pie I used to eat in North Finland during the year I spent there. *Isoaidin Pulla*, or Grandmother's Pulla, is a sweet, enriched bread dough which the Finns top with some of their plentiful berries, such as blueberries, lingonberries or Arctic brambles. *Pulla* is Finnish for bun, and theirs is flavoured usually with ground cardamom; it is also rolled up, Chelsea bun-style, with lots of butter, sugar and cinnamon. To finish off this pudding, the cheese topping on the pizza is Mascarpone, the most delicious, calorie-laden cream cheese from Italy. This is a menu full of fun, full of taste.

ONLY THE PIZZA DOUGH CAN BE PREPARED IN ADVANCE (IT CAN PROVE IN THE FRIDGE OVERNIGHT), ALTHOUGH THE BARLEY RAGOUT COULD BE REHEATED, IF NECESSARY

A vigorous red wine is best to match the strong goat's cheese and aubergine flavours – for example, a Chianti or Zinfandel. This can also be drunk throughout the main course, as the earthy flavours of the mushrooms would combine well. For the 'fun' pudding, a sweet Vouvray would be delicious.

Aubergine and Goat's Cheese Layer

2 large aubergines
2 red peppers
extra virgin olive oil
4 slices fresh goat's cheese (from a round, or individual 'crottin')
40 ml (8 tsp) pesto sauce
60 ml (4 tbsp) shredded rocket, or lamb's lettuce
90 ml (6 tbsp) vinaigrette (made with best olive oil and balsamic vinegar)
polenta croûtons

1. Cut aubergines into thick slices (you need 2 fairly uniform slices per person), sprinkle with salt, leave to sweat for 1–2 hours. Pat dry with paper towel.

2. Grill or roast peppers (under very hot grill or in very hot oven) until skin is charred and blistered. Place in polythene bag, seal and leave for about 20 minutes. Remove skin, cut flesh into strips and mix with a little olive oil.

3. Heat some oil in a frying pan and fry aubergines until golden brown (about 2 minutes each side). Pat dry with paper towel.

4. Place aubergines on individual plates, top with cheese. Working quickly, cover with some red pepper strips, then 5 ml (1 tsp) pesto. Sprinkle rocket or lettuce over, then vinaigrette.

5. Top with aubergine slice, then more pesto, then rocket or lettuce. Place a polenta croûton on the 'summit', and serve at once.

NONE OF THE STARTER CAN BE FROZEN

Barley and Wild Mushroom Ragout

200 g (7 oz) pearl barley
50 g (2 oz) unsalted butter
1–2 cloves garlic, peeled, chopped
200 g (7 oz) shallots or onions, peeled, chopped
225 g (8 oz) mixed fresh mushrooms (chanterelles, ceps, or cultivated shiitake, oyster)
15 g (½ oz) dried morels
4 ml (¾ tsp) salt
4 ml (¾ tsp) black pepper
2 sprigs thyme
300 ml (10 fl oz) vegetable stock
(fresh thyme leaves, to garnish)

1. Soak morels and any other dried mushrooms in a little of the stock, for about half an hour.

2. Melt butter in casserole, sauté shallots and garlic for 5 minutes.

3. Slice fresh mushrooms thickly. Squeeze dried ones with your hand, reserving the liquor. Slice these and add all mushrooms to pan; cook for 3 minutes.

4. Add barley, seasoning, stock and mushroom liquor. Mix well, bring to the boil and cover.

5. Transfer to preheated oven 160° C (325° F/Gas 3) for 40 minutes, or until liquid is absorbed.

6. Sprinkle with fresh thyme leaves and serve, with leeks, at once.

Leeks in Warm Vinaigrette

4 young leeks
5 ml (1 tsp) Dijon mustard
15 ml (1 tbsp) blueberry vinegar
freshly ground pepper
coarse sea salt
45–75 ml (3–5 tbsp) olive oil

1. Cut the leeks diagonally into slices and steam for about 2 minutes, until just cooked.

2. **For the vinaigrette:** mix together the mustard, vinegar, salt and pepper. Whisk in enough oil to give a thick emulsion.

3. Once the leeks are well drained, toss immediately in the vinaigrette and serve. (It is actually the vegetables which are warm, not the vinaigrette; the heat transfers to the dressing.)

NONE OF THE MAIN COURSE CAN BE FROZEN

Blackcurrant Pizza with Mascarpone

PIZZA

25 g (1 oz) butter, cubed
225 g (8 oz) strong white flour
15 g (½ oz) fresh yeast (if using dried yeast, follow guidance
on packet)
90 ml (3½ fl oz) milk, lukewarm
15 ml (1 tbsp) caster sugar
5 ml (1 tsp) crushed cardamom
15 g (½ oz) melted butter

TOPPING

325 g (12 oz) blackcurrants (if frozen, drain well)
15 ml (1 tbsp) cornflour
100 g (4 oz) soft brown sugar

TO FINISH

60 ml (4 tbsp) Mascarpone, beaten until smooth. (Icing sugar can
be added, to sweeten.)
30 ml (2 tbsp) sifted icing sugar

1. Mix yeast with the milk and 10 ml (½ tbsp) of the sugar. Stir and leave for 10 minutes.

2. With fingertips, rub butter into flour. Add remaining 10 ml (½ tbsp) sugar and cardamom.

3. Pour yeast mixture on to flour and combine with spoon until well mixed. Turn on to board and knead until dough is smooth and elastic.

4. Place in large clean bowl, cover with clingfilm and put somewhere warm (airing cupboard, for example) for 1–2 hours, until well risen.

5. Knock back dough, re-knead briefly.

6. Roll out to fit 25 cm (10 inch) buttered round tin (the dough should be about 1 cm (½ inch) thick). Make sure it covers not only the base but the sides too.

7. Cover and allow to rise for half an hour.

8. Mix blackcurrants with cornflour and brown sugar. Spread over pizza base. Brush edges with melted butter.

9. Bake in preheated oven 220°C (425°F/Gas 7) for about 20 minutes, or until risen and puffy.

10. Sprinkle with sifted icing sugar whenever it emerges from the oven. Serve hot with a dollop of Mascarpone cheese (or Greek yoghurt if you prefer a lower fat content).

THE PIZZA DOUGH CAN BE FROZEN, EITHER ALREADY RISEN OR BEFORE THE PROVING STAGE. DO NOT FREEZE WITH THE BERRIES ON TOP

FRANCES ATKINS left her English roots to settle in Aberfeldy, Perthshire, where she and her husband own Farleyer House Hotel. She has become a devotee of what Scotland has to offer in the way of produce, and has developed her own style of cuisine around this. She is delighted to offer vegetarian dishes alongside local fish, game and meat on her menu.

Photograph © *The Scotsman*

A Puff-Pastry Vegetable Sausage with Tomato Coulis and an Orange and Basil Salad

SERVES 4

VEGETABLE SAUSAGE

100 g (4 oz) fine breadcrumbs
50 g (2 oz) Gruyère cheese, finely grated
450 g (1 lb) mixed chopped vegetables (mushrooms, carrots, leeks, onions, beans)
5 ml (1 tsp) garlic, peeled, crushed
10 ml (¾ tbsp) olive oil
15 g (½ oz) caraway seeds
25 g (1 oz) pinenuts or raisins
zest of 1 orange
½ beaten egg
seasoning
100 g (4 oz) puff-pastry
1 sheet filo pastry
knob of butter, melted

1. Heat oil in pan with garlic and cook vegetables lightly, in order to retain their crunch. Cool.

2. Add vegetables to breadcrumbs with cheese, pinenuts or raisins, orange zest and seasoning. Bind together with egg.

3. Roll into sausage shape.

4. Roll out puff-pastry thinly. Wrap up sausage, then rewrap in filo pastry. Brush all over with melted butter.

5. Cook in preheated oven 200°C (400°F/Gas 6) for about 20 minutes. Slice and serve on tomato coulis, with orange and basil salad.

TOMATO COULIS

450 g (1 lb) tomatoes
1 clove garlic, peeled, crushed
10 ml (¾ tbsp) sugar
salt, pepper
dash soy sauce
1 medium onion, finely chopped
olive oil
sherry

1. Heat pan with a dash of oil. Sauté onion and garlic, add chopped tomato, seasoning and soy sauce. Cook well and cool.

2. Blend in food processor, then sieve.

3. Add sugar and little sherry to correct consistency.

ORANGE AND BASIL SALAD

1 orange
mixed salad leaves
spring onions, finely chopped
large bunch of fresh basil
2 ml (½ tsp) mustard
10 ml (¾ tbsp) wine vinegar
25 ml (1 ½ tbsp) oil to mix

1. Segment orange, saving all juice.

2. Mix together mustard and vinegar to make paste. Add oil and orange juice to taste.

3. Place orange, chopped basil and salad leaves together and pour over dressing.

Menu

Chicken Liver Parcels
with Cumberland Sauce

• •

Orange Zest Pasta with Scallops
Fennel & Sweet Cicely Salad

• •

Brioche Summer Pudding

Chapter Six

ALTHOUGH NOT KNOWN FOR PARSIMONY, I ALWAYS GAIN GREAT satisfaction from making inexpensive food items into something which looks extravagant. In this menu, therefore, there is evidence of the infamous Scottish thrift. Take half a pound of chicken livers, which are delightfully cheap, a few other ingredients, and you have a splendid starter. Home-made Cumberland Sauce is tangy and delicious, and keeps for several days in the fridge.

The main course does not look cheap; and yet you need only a few scallops – say, 3 or 4 – per person. Pasta can, if you want, always bulk out a meal, so you can cut down on expensive proteins to go with it. This particular pasta is flavoured with orange zest. It is unusual not only because of the combination of orange with pasta, but also because it actually tastes of orange. So often coloured pasta does not taste of spinach or tomato, but simply looks green or red. This recipe retains its citrus flavour even after cooking. Try to avoid frozen scallops if possible since they retain excess liquid which impairs their texture on cooking. The fennel salad has a dressing of olive oil with freshly squeezed orange juice, which goes well with the orange pasta. Sweet cicely is an old-fashioned herb, which is found wild in southern Scotland. Its rather sweet anise flavour blends perfectly well with the fennel and it also looks wonderful with its attractive, lacy leaves. Apart from salads, it is also used with stewed rhubarb or fruit salads.

The last recipe is summer pudding with a difference, a variation on the classical dessert: instead of having white bread as the base, brioche is used. It holds its shape well and is sweet without having the sugary aftertaste of an alternative summer pudding, made with trifle sponges. Soft fruits are another inexpensive item, certainly in Scotland, where you can pick your own. Every summer, as a young child, I used to pick raspberries and blackcurrants in my parent's garden. Then when I was slightly older, I would go to stay with my aunt near Dundee and go 'to the berries', to pick raspberries, strawberries and currants. We would drop them into 'luggies' (buckets), which were attached at the waist. I never became tired of tasting the berries as I worked. Their memorable succulence is not ruined in this recipe by over-elaboration. It appeals to all ages in its refreshing simplicity.

THE CHICKEN LIVER PARCELS CAN BE PREPARED AND KEPT IN THE FRIDGE FOR UP TO 6 HOURS. THE CUMBERLAND SAUCE CAN KEEP FOR 4 TO 5 DAYS. THE PASTA CAN BE PRE-PARED IN ADVANCE AND FROZEN OR DRIED. THE SALAD DRESSING AND THE SUMMER PUDDING SHOULD BE MADE THE DAY BEFORE

Dry white wine could be served throughout this menu – for example, a white Bordeaux or Pouilly-Fumé. An alternative for the main course might be a less dry white, for example, Gewurz-traminer. The fruity pudding would be wonderful with a young Sauternes wine.

Chicken Liver Parcels with Cumberland Sauce

CHICKEN LIVER FILLING

225 g (8 oz) chicken livers, trimmed
2–3 shallots, peeled, chopped
1 clove garlic, peeled, crushed
2 rashers unsmoked streaky bacon, chopped
25 g (1 oz) unsalted butter
75 ml (3 fl oz) double cream
2 sprigs of fresh thyme
salt, pepper
15 ml (1 tbsp) brandy

1. Heat butter in pan, add garlic, shallots, bacon. Sauté until soft. Add livers, sauté on a high heat for 2 to 3 minutes. (Stand back: the livers splatter dangerously!)

2. Add thyme, salt, pepper and brandy, then cool for 10 minutes.

3. Purée in food processor, adding cream gradually. Taste for seasoning, then turn into a bowl and chill well.

CHICKEN LIVER PARCELS

4 large sheets of filo pastry
4 large oyster or shiitake mushrooms, wiped, sliced
75 g (3 oz) unsalted butter, melted
10 ml (2 tsp) sesame seeds
chicken liver mixture
salt, pepper

TO FINISH

4 sprigs fresh thyme

1. Cook mushrooms for 2 minutes in 15 g (½ oz) butter. Drain and pat dry.

2. Keeping other pastry sheets covered as you work, brush one sheet of filo with butter. Fold over to make rectangle, then paint with butter again.

3. Place 15 ml (1 tbsp) of the chicken liver mixture on to the middle, then place some mushrooms on top. Season well. Place another 15 ml (1 tbsp) of the mixture on the top.

4. Roll filo over and tuck under, like a little parcel, brushing butter on edges to seal.

5. Sprinkle over sesame seeds and place, sealed side underneath, on buttered baking tray. Refrigerate for an hour (or longer) and bake in preheated oven 200°C (400°F/Gas 6) for 20 minutes.

6. Serve piping hot with a pool of Cumberland Sauce and a sprig of thyme to garnish.

CUMBERLAND SAUCE

1 orange
½ lemon
2 ml (½ tsp) dry mustard
50 ml (2 fl oz) port
30 ml (2 tbsp) redcurrant jelly
2 ml (½ tsp) salt
freshly ground pepper
10 ml (½ tbsp) red wine vinegar

1. Thinly pare rind from orange and lemon and cut into slices. Boil in pan of boiling water for 4–5 minutes. Refresh in cold water and drain.

2. Squeeze juice from orange and lemon. Mix this with mustard and vinegar in pan, then add port, redcurrant jelly, salt, pepper, orange and lemon rinds.

3. Place over medium heat, bring to boil, stirring until jelly melts. Reduce to low heat, simmer for 20 minutes until slightly thick. (The end consistency is more runny than thick, however.)

4. Strain into clean bowl, leave to cool, cover and refrigerate.

THE CHICKEN LIVER MIXTURE CAN BE FROZEN AND
DEFROSTED WELL BEFORE USE

Orange Zest Pasta with Scallops

ORANGE ZEST PASTA

225 g (8 oz) strong white flour
5 ml (1 tsp) salt
finely grated zest of 2 large oranges
2 eggs, large

1. Make as referred to in Chapter Two, mixing all ingredients in food processor, then resting for 30 minutes before rolling out. Roll to penultimate setting. Flour lightly and leave sheets to dry for another 30 minutes, then cut into spaghetti. Ease gently apart as you hang it to dry.

2. Either cook immediately in boiling salted water with a little oil in it, for less than 1 minute; or freeze, once dried. If frozen, cook from frozen for 2 to 3 minutes.

3. Once drained, toss in some olive oil and grind black pepper over.

SCALLOPS

700 g (1 ½ lb) fresh scallops (about 3 to 4 per person)
salt, pepper
30 ml (2 tbsp) olive oil
glass dry white wine

1. Clean scallops by removing any dark threads (your fishmonger should do this). If necessary, wash briefly and pat dry.

2. Place in bowl, season with salt and pepper, then turn in 15 ml (1 tbsp) of the olive oil. Make sure they are covered well with the oil, then cover with clingfilm and refrigerate for a few hours.

3. Bring to room temperature for 30 minutes then heat remaining oil in heavy-based pan until very hot. Place scallops in and cook, turning once, for no more than 3 minutes (less if some are not so plump). Do this in batches; you should not crowd the pan.

4. Remove from pan and keep warm. Now pour off any milky-looking liquids from pan, then deglaze pan with the wine, scraping up the scallop juices, reduce a little, season and serve (strained if necessary) over the scallops.

(This is a very simple sauce, as the orange pasta is such a delicate flavour and should not be overpowered by rich sauces. If you like, either a little beurre blanc or a warmed olive oil sauce can be served separately.)

Fennel and Sweet Cicely Salad

1–2 bulbs of fennel
1 frisée lettuce, washed
1 bunch of sweet cicely
60 ml (4 tbsp) extra virgin olive oil
30 ml (2 tbsp) freshly squeezed orange juice
(not from a carton)
salt, pepper

1. Cut away coarse outer leaves from fennel, then chop inner leaves into slices or chunks. Place prepared frisée in a large salad bowl, place fennel on top, then roughly tear the sweet cicely and strew over the top.

2. Shake the oil, juice, salt and pepper together in screw-top jar and pour over salad. Toss well and serve with the scallops and pasta.

ONLY THE PASTA CAN BE FROZEN

Brioche Summer Pudding

1 x 450 g (1 lb) brioche (I use the rectangular loaf-shape one from Marks & Spencer)
450 g (1 lb) mixed berries (redcurrants, brambles, blackcurrants, gooseberries, blueberries)
75 g (3 oz) caster sugar
25 g (1 oz) unsalted butter
(1 x 450 g (1 lb) loaf tin, lined with clingfilm)

1. Place berries and sugar in heavy-based pan and cook very gently for 3–4 minutes, until fruit is softened and sugar dissolved.

2. Slice brioche horizontally into 1 cm (½ inch) slices and spread one side of each with butter.

3. Place one slice, buttered side up, in base of tin. Spoon fruit, with slotted spoon, on top, then top with second slice of brioche. Add more fruit, then another slice of brioche.

4. Add the last of the fruit, the fourth slice of brioche (this time buttered side down), and cover with some of the fruit juices (just enough to soak in lightly, not flood!).

5. Boil up remaining juices, reduce until thick and reserve, to serve with the pudding.

6. Cover the pudding with clingfilm, place a suitable weight on top (a tin is good), and place in the fridge overnight (minimum of 12 hours).

7. Turn out and serve in thick slices with Greek yoghurt or thick cream and reduced fruit juices.

DO NOT FREEZE THIS PUDDING

CHRISTOPHER TROTTER, chef partner of The Grange Inn, St Andrews, is an advocate of organic food and has a preference for cooking with natural ingredients in a simple manner, so their natural flavours emerge triumphantly.

Scallops with Fresh Ginger and Leek

SERVES 4

2 scallops per person for starter *or* 3 as main course
1 cm (½ inch) peeled, grated, fresh ginger
100 g (4 oz) butter
dash white wine
300 ml (10 fl oz) fish stock
lemon juice
2 leeks, cut into fine strips about 5 cm (2 inch) long

1. In an open shallow pan over a low heat, melt 50 g (2 oz) butter and cook scallops gently until barely cooked. Add their roes at the last minute as they cook more quickly (about 3 minutes altogether).

2. Remove them from the pan and keep warm between 2 plates so they do not dry out.

3. Add the grated ginger to the pan and stir to fry lightly, which helps to bring out the flavour.

4. Add the wine and stock and simmer gently to reduce by half.

5. Slice the scallops across the grain into three or four slices, leaving the roes whole.

6. As the sauce thickens, add the leek and allow to go limp, then swirl in the remaining 50 g (2 oz) butter in knobs away from the heat so as to incorporate it into the liquid without boiling.

7. Add a touch of lemon juice and check for seasoning. Return the scallops to the pan, heat through and serve immediately. Try to pile them so they rise off the plate and the leek is well mixed through, with the sauce around.

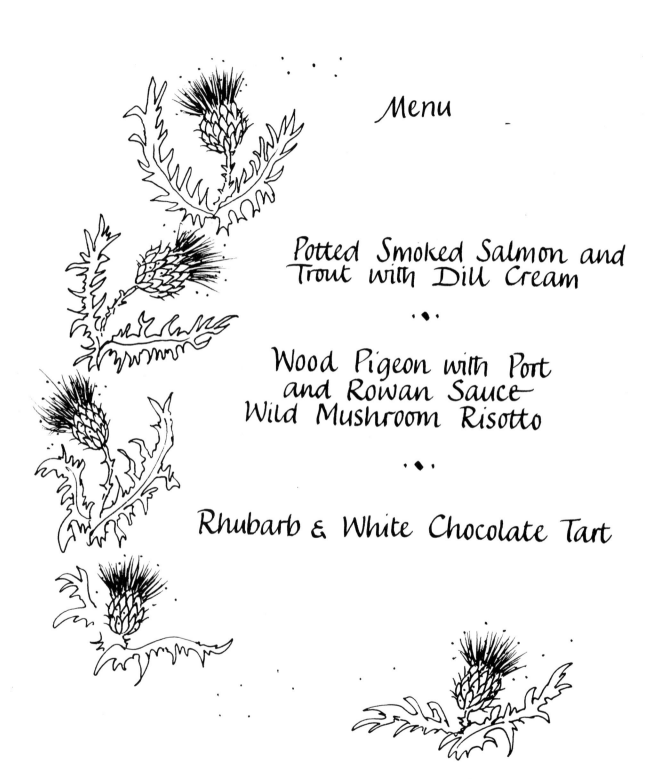

Menu

Potted Smoked Salmon and
Trout with Dill Cream

• ◆ •

Wood Pigeon with Port
and Rowan Sauce
Wild Mushroom Risotto

• ◆ •

Rhubarb & White Chocolate Tart

Chapter Seven

THERE ARE STRONG SCOTTISH FLAVOURS IN THIS MENU – PIGEON, rowans, wild mushrooms – alongside the more delicate, yet equally typical, flavours of salmon, trout and rhubarb.

The starter is versatile, as quantities of each fish can be inter-changed. I would recommend, however, always using some smoked fish to accompany the fresh fish for a greater depth of flavour. It is essential to taste as you prepare this, for certain smoked fish are saltier than others. If you use smoked salmon off-cuts, make sure there are no hard, rubbery pieces which will refuse to blend in the processor. Off-cuts are not ideal for the garnish, once the ramekin is inverted.

Wood-pigeon has no close season, so it is available all year. Ensure the birds are young for this recipe; a farmed squab would be suitable otherwise. 'Doocots', or dove-cots, have been an integral part of the Scottish countryside over the centuries and pigeons were everyday fare. Nowadays, they are not only inexpensive, but also provide a lean, healthy meat. It is easy to remove the breasts with a very sharp knife, which you should keep as close to the breast bone as possible. Use the remaining carcass for your stock (roast the bones, for a dark stock). The vivid red berries of the rowan or moun-tain ash are a common sight all over Scotland. They should be picked whenever they ripen (in September), for they are much sought after by birds and jelly-makers alike! The bitter-sweetness of rowan jelly is perfect with game. The wild mushroom risotto can stand on its own, as a vegetarian main dish, with some grated Parmesan stirred in at the end. The addition of a green vegetable, such as Savoy cabbage, would provide a bright splash of colour to the plate.

The pudding is a ginger pastry crust (which can also be varied by using ten gingernut biscuits and 50 g (2 oz) butter to make a biscuit crumb crust) and a filling reminiscent of a baked cheese-cake. The origins of this are, again, from Finland, where '*rahkapiirakka*' or cream cheese pie is a family favourite. *Rahka* is the rich cream cheese the Finns use in the mixture to fill shortcrust pastry, or, more typically, a rich sweet sweet bread dough. I have added rhubarb (for its splendid pink colour) and, to counteract its tartness – white chocolate. The combination is unusual (rhubarb is more often combined with orange or ginger or vanilla), but they work exceptionally well together. Taste before you bake, as forced (early) rhubarb needs less sugar than main crop varieties.

THE STARTER CAN BE PREPARED UP TO 12 HOURS IN ADVANCE, BUT THE MAIN COURSE MUST BE COOKED AT THE LAST MINUTE (APART FROM YOUR STOCK). THE PUDDING CAN BE MADE A FEW HOURS PRIOR TO SERVING, ALTHOUGH IT TASTES BEST WHEN SLIGHTLY WARM

The fishy starter is best accompanied by a New Zealand Fumé Blanc or a Sancerre. The strong flavour of wood-pigeon could handle a lively red – a Chianti Classico or Californian Cabernet. For the sweet tart, a Monbazillac would be wonderful.

AUBERGINE AND GOAT'S CHEESE LAYER WITH POLENTA
CROÛTON

BRIOCHE SUMMER PUDDING WITH GREEK YOGHURT

POTTED SMOKED SALMON AND TROUT WITH DILL CREAM

MINT COUSCOUS WITH LAMB

Potted Smoked Salmon and Trout with Dill Cream

POTTED SMOKED SALMON AND TROUT

1 rainbow trout (about 325 g (12 oz)), gutted, scaled, cleaned
court bouillon (I flavour mine with dill or parsley stalks, lemon
juice, white wine, and peppercorns)
100g (4 oz) smoked salmon
2 shallots, peeled, chopped
50 ml (2 fl oz) crème fraîche
50 g (2 oz) unsalted butter, softened
½ lemon, squeezed
pinch cayenne
salt, pepper

DILL CREAM

125 ml (4 fl oz) crème fraîche
10–15 ml (2–3 tsp) freshly chopped dill
½ lemon, squeezed
salt, pepper
(dill fronds, to garnish)

1. Poach trout, cool and flake off flesh.

2. Put in food processor with shallots, crème fraîche, butter and 50 g (2 oz) smoked salmon.

3. Season to taste with lemon juice, cayenne, salt, pepper and spoon into clingfilm-lined small ramekins.

4. Cover with clingfilm, refrigerate for a few hours.

5. **For cream:** combine everything together in bowl.

6. Turn out the ramekins on to a plate. 'Wrap' the remaining smoked salmon, sliced thinly, around the potted fish. Pour the cream around and garnish with dill fronds.

7. Serve with thinly sliced brown Melba toast or thin oatcakes.

NONE OF THE STARTER CAN BE FROZEN

Wood-pigeon with Port and Rowan Sauce

4 young wood-pigeon
15 ml (1 tbsp) olive oil
15 ml (1 tbsp) hazelnut oil
15 g (½ oz) unsalted butter
salt, pepper
150 ml (5 fl oz) port
450 ml (15 fl oz) dark game stock
15 ml (1 tbsp) rowan jelly
lemon juice (freshly squeezed)

1. Remove breasts from pigeons, and skin. Cover with oils, cover and refrigerate for a few hours.

2. Heat butter in frying pan, add breasts, season lightly and brown on both sides (this takes about 1 minute altogether, with fat very hot).

3. Transfer to lightly buttered baking tray and bake in preheated oven 230°C (450°F/Gas 8) for about 8 minutes (depending on size). Remove and rest 5–10 minutes, in warm place. Cut into slices and serve with sauce around.

4. **For sauce:** boil port and stock together until reduced to 150 ml (5 fl oz) or slightly thickened. Add rowan jelly, stir until melted. Taste for seasoning, add lemon juice (a dash, to sharpen it), and serve around the breasts.

Wild Mushroom Risotto

25 g (1 oz) dried ceps
30 ml (2 tbsp) olive oil
1 garlic clove, peeled, crushed
2-3 shallots, peeled, chopped
275 g (10 oz) arborio rice
175 g (6 oz) fresh mushrooms (horn of plenty, chanterelles, ceps;
or large flat cap)
150 ml (5 fl oz) dry white wine
900 ml (30 fl oz) good chicken stock
25 g (1 oz) butter
30 ml (2 tbsp) freshly chopped parsley and thyme, mixed

1. Soak dried mushrooms in the wine for half an hour.

2. Heat oil in pan, sauté garlic and shallots for 2-3 minutes.

3. Drain and slice ceps (reserve liquid). Add these and other mushrooms to pan, fry for 2-3 minutes. Remove from pan with slotted spoon.

4. Add rice to pan, stir well then pour in cep liquid, bring to boil. Simmer over low heat.

5. Add stock gradually, stirring as liquid is absorbed. Cook gently, adding stock as necessary (about 15 minutes) until risotto is tender.

6. Remove from heat, add mushrooms, butter and half of herbs; season to taste. Cover and leave for 5 minutes, then serve with remaining herbs sprinkled over, to accompany pigeon.

THE GAME STOCK CAN BE FROZEN; NOTHING ELSE FROM THE MAIN COURSE CAN BE FROZEN

Rhubarb and White Chocolate Tart

PASTRY

175 g (6 oz) plain flour, sifted
pinch salt
50 g (2 oz) caster sugar
75 g (3 oz) unsalted butter, cubed
1 egg yolk, medium
2 ml (½ tsp) ground ginger
30 ml (2 tbsp) water

FILLING

60 g (2 ½ oz) good white chocolate, grated
225 g (8 oz) young rhubarb (preferably 'Champagne' variety, for
its colour)
25 g (1 oz) light muscovado sugar
15 ml (1 tbsp) water
100 g (4 oz) quark
100 g (4 oz) curd or cream cheese
1 egg, large
40 g (1 ½ oz) light muscovado sugar (if older rhubarb, use more
sugar)

1. **For pastry:** place flour, ginger, salt and sugar into food processor and process for a couple of seconds. Add butter and process until mixture resembles breadcrumbs. Add egg yolk and sufficient water to bind, until mixture 'balls'. Cover in clingfilm and refrigerate for half an hour.

2. Chop rhubarb into small pieces and cook with water and sugar for 10–15 minutes until tender. Drain very well. Cool and mash or purée.

3. Beat quark with cream cheese and sugar until smooth. Add egg then cooled rhubarb purée (either fold in thoroughly or leave swirled effect).

4. Roll out pastry to fit 20 cm (8 inch) loose-bottom, lightly greased, deep tart tin. (There should be enough pastry left to make 3–4 jam tarts for the children!)

5. Prick well, then refrigerate for 45 minutes (overnight if possible; this prevents shrinkage).

6. Bake blind in preheated oven 200°C (400°F/Gas 6) for 15 minutes with baking beans and foil; then a further 5–10 minutes without.

7. Cool, then spread grated chocolate all over base. Pour rhubarb mixture carefully over top, trying to keep it within pastry sides. Level out top and bake in middle of preheated oven 190°C (375°F/Gas 5) for about 45–50 minutes, or until just set. Wait half an hour then remove sides, slide on to serving plate and serve at room temperature or slightly warm.

DO NOT FREEZE THE TART

RUTH HADLEY has been chef and proprietor of The Cross, Kingus-sie, since 1982. Totally self-taught, her food is sophisticated yet homely. Her smoked salmon recipe shows how simple gourmet fare can be.

Prawn and Smoked Salmon Parcels

SERVES 6

450 g (1 lb) best-quality prawns, cooked
225 ml (8 fl oz) natural yoghurt
juice of half a lemon
fresh dill, finely chopped
seasoning
6 thin slices smoked salmon (large enough to line and top
ramekins)

1. Line six small ramekins with thin slices of smoked salmon (enough for an overhang too).

2. Roughly chop the prawns and place in a bowl with the remaining ingredients, mix well and season to taste.

3. Fill the lined ramekins with the mixture and cover with the over-hangs of salmon. Top each ramekin with clingfilm and chill for 3–4 hours.

4. Turn out on to a plate and garnish with salad, watercress, cucumber or avocado.

Chapter Eight

RENAISSANCE OF TRADITIONAL FARE IS THE THEME FOR THIS MENU. The starter is a modern version of the old Scottish favourite, 'Ham and Haddie', which is a smoked haddock (often Finnan haddock) with a slice of smoked ham. A poached egg on top makes a complete dish for family high tea. As a starter, try to buy small fillets of smoked haddock and ensure they are undyed; the yellow dye is unnatural and inessential. Parma ham is a perfect partner, and if you are lucky enough to have lovage growing in your garden, a few leaves of this old-fashioned herb (which is reminiscent of celery) enhances the entire dish. Potato scones (or tattie scones, as they are more commonly known) are also a tea-time favourite, either freshly made or grilled the next day. Served plain or topped with butter, they are good either with jam or honey, or to accompany savoury dishes like bacon and eggs.

Mint with lamb is traditional, as are the accompanying vegetables. By incorporating couscous, a staple of North Africa, however, a Mediterranean flavour is introduced. Usually, the grain is steamed and served with spicy stews. I remember, as an au pair in Provence, watching the huge *couscousière* being filled with all the delicious vegetables and meats in the morning, and later the couscous added to the steamer section. It was the cause of some mirth when I had my first taste of Harissa, the accompanying fiery chilli sauce – a volcanic taste sensation to a Scot reared on mince and tatties! Most packets of couscous sold in this country give simple cooking instructions; a delicious couscous salad with lots of garlic, mint, parsley and vinaigrette is a summer favourite in our family.

The tradition of baking in Scotland is still very much alive. Gingerbread has always been one of the old favourites. This recipe is unusual as it contains rum, which makes it moist and delicious, but decidedly adult-oriented. It is cut into rounds (there is no waste; a superb ginger trifle will be next day's pudding) and topped with

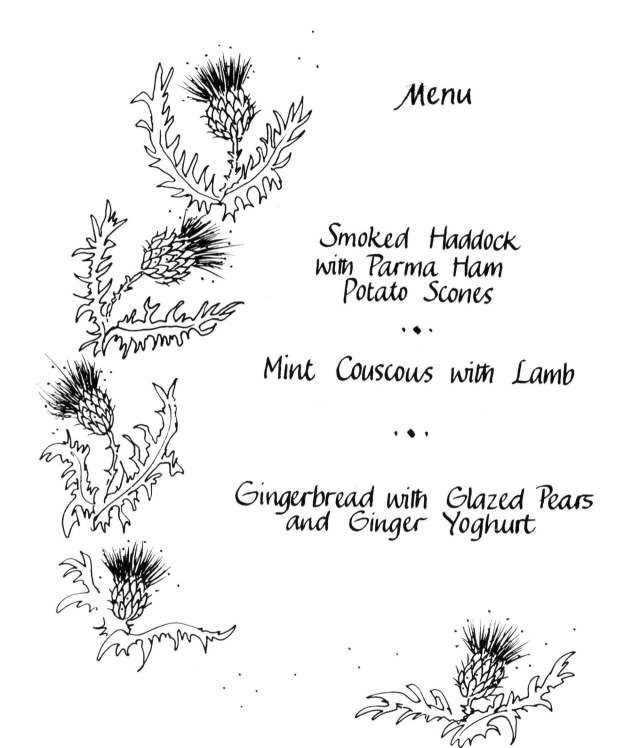

Menu

**Smoked Haddock
with Parma Ham
Potato Scones**

• •

Mint Couscous with Lamb

• •

**Gingerbread with Glazed Pears
and Ginger Yoghurt**

pears, butter and sugar, which caramelise under the grill. A good accompaniment is ginger-flavoured yoghurt or, if you have time, a real custard (crème anglaise) made with pure vanilla pod, is sensational.

THE POTATO SCONES CAN BE COOKED IN ADVANCE,
REFRIGERATED AND GRILLED AS REQUIRED. THE LAMB
SHOULD BE MARINATED OVERNIGHT, AND THE GINGERBREAD
MADE 2–3 DAYS IN ADVANCE

The smoky flavours of the fish and the ham would be enhanced by a Pouilly-Fumé or perhaps an Australian Chardonnay. The couscous and lamb dish taste best served with a dry young red – for example, a Minervois or Corbières. For the gingerbread, a rich, honeyed wine, like Malmsey Madeira, would be perfect.

Smoked Haddock with Parma Ham

4 small fillets smoked haddock
4 thin slices Parma ham
175 ml (6 fl oz) milk
40 g (1 ½ oz) unsalted butter
60 ml (4 tbsp) double cream
small bunch fresh lovage (or flat parsley), chopped, and 4 leaves
reserved for garnish
freshly ground pepper

1. Poach haddock in milk, with 15 g (½ oz) butter (cover with lid). Remove and keep warm. (This takes about 3–4 minutes.)

2. Melt remaining butter, add lovage (parsley), then cream and 60 ml (4 tbsp) of the poaching liquor. Bring to boil then reduce until thick. (This takes 2–3 minutes.) Season to taste (no salt should be required, as the haddock is salty).

3. Arrange haddock on plates. Slide the Parma ham (torn into strips or whole) into the remaining poaching liquor (turn over once) to warm through (this takes only seconds). Place on top of haddock, pour sauce over and decorate with lovage leaf (or parsley).

Potato Scones

1 large potato, peeled, boiled
40–50g (1 ½–2 oz) plain flour, sifted
50 g (2 oz) melted butter
salt, freshly ground pepper

1. Mash potato with half of the butter while still warm. Add enough flour to combine well without becoming too dry. (Using a floury potato like Maris Piper means you need less flour.) Season very well.

2. On floured board, roll out to 0.6 cm (¼ inch) and cut into circles, then quarters. Prick with a fork, sprinkle a little flour over surface.

3. Heat remaining butter in a large frying pan (or ideally, a hot girdle) and cook for about 3 minutes each side until browned and firm; drain on kitchen paper.

4. Serve warm, freshly cooked, or (I think this is even better) toasted under a grill.

ONLY THE POTATO SCONES CAN BE FROZEN. GRILL FROM FROZEN FOR ABOUT 5 MINUTES

Mint Couscous with Lamb

700 g (1 ½ lb) boned, rolled shoulder of lamb

MARINADE

3 cloves garlic, peeled, crushed
1 large bunch fresh mint
salt, pepper
50 ml (2 fl oz) olive oil

COUSCOUS

450 g (1 lb) couscous
2 ml (½ tsp) salt
50 g (2 oz) butter
1 small leek, cleaned, diced finely
1 large carrot, peeled, diced finely
225 g (8 oz) turnip (swede), peeled, diced finely
1 large bunch fresh mint, chopped

SAUCE

15 ml (1 tbsp) olive oil
1 onion, peeled, chopped
1 carrot, peeled, chopped
1 stick celery, chopped
2 large tomatoes, chopped
2–3 sprigs thyme
Half bottle dry white wine
Harissa (or Tabasco): 5–6 dashes, depending on how hot
you like it
fresh mint leaves, to garnish

1. Combine garlic, mint and seasoning in food processor. Add enough olive oil to combine, until consistency of thick cream. Prick lamb all over with fine skewer, and pour marinade all over; rub in well. Cover and leave overnight (or 8 hours minimum).

2. Next day, place meat (which you have brought to room tempera-ture for an hour or so) in preheated oven 200°C (400°F/Gas 6) and roast for 45 minutes until still pink inside. Baste frequently while roasting. Remove to warm place, cover and leave to rest for 10–15 minutes before carving into slices.

3. **For sauce:** sauté carrots, onion and celery in oil until softened. Add tomatoes and sweat. Add thyme and wine, then reduce to half (about 10 minutes). Sieve, season, then whisk in the Harissa (Tabasco). Taste as you go, to determine how much to add. Keep warm.

4. **For couscous:** heat butter and sauté turnip, carrot and leek. Cover and cook over low heat until just done (about 10–15 minutes). Shake pan frequently.

5. Place couscous in bowl and pour in sufficient boiling water to just cover. Fork through, then place doubled tea towel tightly over and leave for 15–20 minutes. Fork through, add salt, then vegeta-bles (and their butter) and the mint. Fluff up with fork again and serve. (If necessary, reheat in oven, well covered.)

6. **To serve:** put couscous on to plate and place slice of lamb on top. Pour some sauce over and decorate with fresh mint.

THE MAIN COURSE CANNOT BE FROZEN

Gingerbread with Glazed Pears and Ginger Yoghurt

GINGERBREAD

150 ml (5 fl oz) milk

150 g (5 oz) (runny) honey (I pour about a third from a new 450 g (1 lb) jar)

100 g (4 oz) caster sugar

1 ml (¼ tsp) ground ginger

1 ml (¼ tsp) ground cinnamon

7 ml (1 ½ tsp) bicarbonate of soda

100 g (4 oz) ground almonds

325 g (12 oz) plain flour, sifted

30 ml (2 tbsp) dark rum

2 egg yolks

PEARS

2 dessert pears (Comice or William are good)

25 g (1 oz) unsalted butter

juice of half lemon

40 g (1 ½ oz) caster sugar

GINGER YOGHURT

300 ml (10 fl oz) thick Greek yoghurt

20-25 ml (4-5 tsp) syrup from jar of stem ginger in syrup

1. **For gingerbread:** butter and line either a 23 cm (9 inch) flan dish *or* a 900 g (2 lb) loaf tin.

2. Bring milk to the boil, remove from heat and add honey, sugar and spices.

3. Place flour, bicarbonate of soda and ground almonds in a bowl, and mix with electric hand-mixer (or very vigorously with hand whisk). Beat mixture slowly as you add the warm milk mixture.

4. Add rum, then egg yolks, mixing well.

5. Pour into prepared tin; leave for 20 minutes then bake in pre-heated oven (middle shelf at 180°C (350°F/Gas 4) for 50–60 minutes) until cooked. Cover with foil towards end.

6. Allow to cool, cover with foil and store for a couple of days (in fridge if necessary).

7. **On day you are using:** for loaf tin, cut into 4 cm (1 ½ inch) slices first. For flan dish, level surface off, then cut out with large pastry cutters 7.6 cm (3 inch) to form 4 flat circles. Keep remaining gingerbread for trifle or other pudding.

8. **For pears:** peel pears, halve and core. Cut into 5 mm (¼ inch) slices, roughly the length of the gingerbread circles. Sprinkle with lemon juice and place in bowl.

9. Sauté pears in pan with butter for 2–3 minutes. Cool, then arrange slices over gingerbread rounds. Sprinkle with caster sugar and heat under hot grill until caramelised (about 3–4 minutes). Serve at once with ginger yoghurt.

10. **For yoghurt:** mix ingredients well together and serve with gingerbread (some of the stem ginger, chopped, can also be added to the yoghurt). If you are serving with a crème anglaise, surround the gingerbread with a 'moat' of the custard on large flat plates.

THE GINGERBREAD CAN BE FROZEN AFTER BAKING

PETER JUKES of The Cellar, Anstruther, is an exponent of light, fresh fish dishes. He uses local Scottish seafood with imagination and simplicity. His smoked haddock omelette epitomises his straightforward approach.

Omelette of Smoked Haddock

SERVES 6 AS A STARTER

125 ml (4 fl oz) white wine
600 ml (1 pint) double cream
(extra cream to hand, if necessary)
12 eggs, well beaten and seasoned
oil, to cook
3 large Finnan haddock
(chervil)

1. Reduce the wine in a heavy-based pan, add the cream then the skin and bone trimmings of the haddock and reduce altogether, for about 10 minutes. (Add more cream if necessary.)

2. Strain the sauce into another heavy-based pan. Cut the haddock fillets into chunks and add to mixture, slowly cooking, on low heat for 10 minutes (with lid on). Gently shake pan, to ensure the contents do not burn. (If you stir, take care not to 'mash' the fish.) Taste for seasoning and add freshly ground pepper, salt, (chopped chervil).

3. Remove this thickish sauce/stew from heat.

4. In a good omelette pan, heat a little oil (swirl round and tip out any excess). Pour in the eggs and cook as for normal omelette, adding plenty of the haddock mixture into the centre of the omelette towards the end. To serve, fold the omelette gently over and slide on to serving plate.

Peter Jukes recommends a good Gewurtztraminer from Alsace as the accompanying wine.

Chapter Nine

THIS IS AN EXTRAVAGANT MENU, WHICH RELIES ON TOP-QUALITY ingredients – strawberries, lamb fillet, best bitter chocolate. The starter is a cold, refreshing soup made primarily with fresh strawberries and mint. Local strawberries have so much more flavour than imported, so June and July are the best months to make this. The use of a well-flavoured, fat-free chicken stock is of paramount importance; no one wants fatty globules in their soup – especially in a chilled soup. The rolls are made with buttermilk, which has sadly lost popularity as a refreshing, healthy drink; it used to be drunk with meals and used in scones and pancakes. Oatmeal is mixed with white flour to produce a rough texture. The rolls should be served warm, to accompany the cold soup.

The lamb is served with a tangy red pepper and champagne sauce; if you can't bear the thought of pouring expensive champagne into a sauce, then a good dry, sparkling cider will do. There are bold colours in this course – the red sauce with the pink meat, the orange of the sweet potato, the vivid green spinach. The contrast of texture is important too, as the sauce and sweet potato are smooth and the spinach still crunchy – not a slimy mass which, despite Popeye connotations, tends to put people off. The first time I had sweet potatoes was at a barbecue in Sydney. Their buttery sweetness matched the grilled 'barbie' meats and the sunshine perfectly. An optional topping to my recipe is brown sugar, butter and cinnamon, which caramelises as it bakes.

The pudding is heavenly – rich dark-chocolate combined with raspberries and white chocolate. The bitter chocolate should have a minimum of 60% cocoa solids, preferably 70%. This ensures an intense flavour which is not overwhelmed by added sugar. The sharpness of the raspberry sauce and the sweetness of the white chocolate sauce contrast perfectly with the marquise, in terms of taste and colour. You could give vent to your artistic imagination

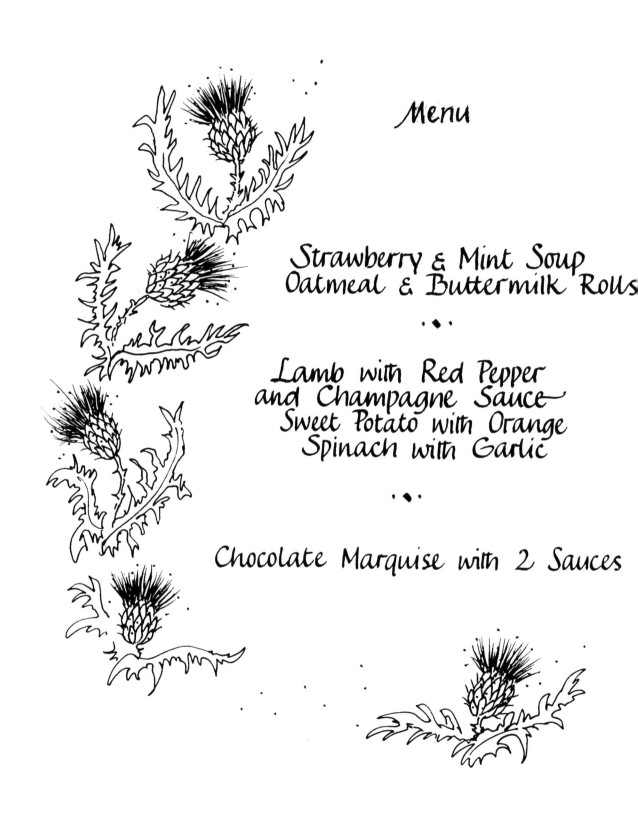

Menu

Strawberry & Mint Soup
Oatmeal & Buttermilk Rolls

❖

Lamb with Red Pepper
and Champagne Sauce
Sweet Potato with Orange
Spinach with Garlic

❖

Chocolate Marquise with 2 Sauces

when it comes to presenting this dish, swirling one sauce into the other, for optimum impact.

THE ROLLS CAN BE MADE EARLIER IN THE DAY AND
REHEATED; THE RED PEPPER SAUCE AND SWEET POTATO CAN
BE PREPARED IN ADVANCE AS CAN THE TWO SWEET SAUCES.
THE CHOCOLATE MARQUISE IS BETTER MADE THE DAY
BEFORE

Since you need champagne for the red pepper sauce, why not drink champagne with the starter – fizz and strawberries always go well. The main dish has a tendency to sweetness, so a peppery wine like Australian Shiraz would be perfect. The chocolate pudding is rich and complex, so, to my mind, wine would be a waste; sparkling mineral water is preferable.

Strawberry and Mint Soup

225 g (8 oz) ripe strawberries
300 ml (10 fl oz) clear chicken stock (not jellied; fat removed)
2 ml (½ tsp) ground ginger
1 ml (¼ tsp) turmeric
300 ml (10 fl oz) natural yoghurt
10–12 large mint leaves
salt, pepper
(extra mint leaves, to garnish)

1. Purée strawberries with the yoghurt and mint. (Strawberries and mint first, then add yoghurt.)

2. Add ginger and turmeric to the stock, heat slowly until the spices dissolve. Cool.

3. Add to the strawberries and yoghurt. Season to taste, then pour into 4 iced soup bowls. Sprinkle with some chopped mint and serve.

Oatmeal and Buttermilk Rolls

25 g (1 oz) fresh yeast. If using dried yeast, follow instructions on
packet
450 ml (15 fl oz) buttermilk, warmed until tepid
5 ml (1 tsp) runny honey, warmed
225 g (8 oz) medium oatmeal
450 g (1 lb) strong white flour
5 ml (1 tsp) salt
2 ml (½ tsp) bicarbonate of soda
50 g (2 oz) melted butter

TO FINISH

25 g (1 oz) melted butter
rolled oats

1. Mix yeast with a little (tepid) buttermilk and honey and leave for
   20 minutes until frothy.

2. Mix all the dry ingredients together, then add remaining buttermilk, yeast mixture and butter.

3. Mix to a dough and turn on to floured board, to knead for
   10 minutes, until dough is smooth.

4. Place in lightly oiled bowl, cover with clingfilm and let it rise for
   1–1½ hours (in warmth).

5. Knock back dough, knead briefly then divide into 16–20 balls.
   Place these on a greased baking sheet and flatten down slightly.
   Brush with melted butter and sprinkle over rolled oats.

6. Cover and place somewhere warm for 1 hour, then bake in preheated oven 220°C (425°F/Gas 7) for 15–20 minutes until brown.

THE SOUP CANNOT BE FROZEN; THE ROLLS FREEZE WELL

Lamb with Red Pepper and Champagne Sauce

SAUCE

2 medium red peppers
½ onion, chopped
125 ml (4 fl oz) champagne
250 ml (8 fl oz) lamb stock, reduced
2–5 ml (½–1 tsp) chilli-flavoured olive oil
salt, pepper
3–4 large basil leaves

MEAT

2 lamb fillets, each weighing about 225–275 g
(8 oz–10 oz)
olive oil

TO FINISH

fresh basil

1. Roast or grill peppers until charred; place in a polythene bag, seal it and leave for about 20 minutes. Then remove skin when cool enough to handle. Chop flesh.

2. Place onion in pan with champagne, bring to the boil then reduce by two-thirds (5–10 minutes).

3. Add peppers and stock and cook for 15–20 minutes until soft. Add chilli oil, then purée and season. (Sieve if fine texture preferred.)

4. Shred basil leaves and stir into sauce; keep warm. (Add more stock if too thick.)

5. **For meat:** rub fillets with olive oil, cover and leave for an hour or so. Heat a little oil in heavy-based frying pan, season lamb then brown in pan, on all sides (about 2–3 minutes).

6. Remove fillets to dish and place in preheated oven 220°C (425°F/Gas 7) for about 5 minutes (depending on thickness of fillets), for a rosy pink lamb. Remove and rest for a couple of minutes.

7. Slice into noisettes and serve with red pepper sauce, garnished with basil.

Sweet Potato with Orange

700 g (1 ½ lb) sweet potatoes, peeled, chopped
50 g (2 oz) butter
salt, pepper
juice and rind of 1 medium orange

1. Boil sweet potatoes, drain and mash with 40 g (1 ½ oz) butter. Season with salt and pepper.

2. Add the orange juice and rind, place in casserole dish with remaining butter on top.

3. Bake in preheated oven 150°C (300°F/Gas 2) until warmed through (about 30 minutes). You can do this before cooking lamb on high temperature, then reheat if necessary.

Spinach with Garlic

450 g (1 lb) young spinach leaves, washed
7.5 ml (½ tbsp) olive oil
7.5 ml (½ tbsp) hazelnut oil
15 g (½ oz) shallots, chopped
2–3 cloves garlic, peeled, crushed
salt, freshly ground pepper

1. Roughly tear spinach leaves. Heat the oils in a pan, add the shallots and garlic and sweat for a couple of minutes.

2. Add the torn spinach (with only the minimum of water clinging to
   their leaves) and cook on high heat (like a stir-fry) for about
   2 minutes, until still crunchy yet cooked. Season well with salt and
   pepper. Serve with lamb.

NONE OF THE MAIN COURSE CAN BE FROZEN

Chocolate Marquise with Two Sauces

CHOCOLATE MARQUISE

200 g (7 oz) best-quality bitter chocolate (Valrhona)
15 ml (1 tbsp) strong coffee
30–45 ml (2–3 tbsp) rum or raspberry liqueur
100 g (4 oz) unsalted butter, softened
100 g (4 oz) caster sugar
30 ml (2 tbsp) cocoa powder, sifted
3 egg yolks
300 ml (10 fl oz) double cream

RASPBERRY SAUCE

450 g (1 lb) raspberries
15 ml (1 tbsp) framboise eau-de-vie
100–150 g (4–5 oz) caster sugar

WHITE CHOCOLATE SAUCE

75 g (3 oz) best-quality white chocolate
300 ml (10 fl oz) single cream
dash of rum or Cointreau

TO FINISH

raspberries
cocoa powder

1. **For marquise:** melt chocolate with coffee and liqueur (over sim-mering water, in a bowl); cool slightly. Beat butter with half the sugar, then fold in cocoa.

2. Whisk egg yolks with remaining sugar; lightly whip cream.

3. Beat chocolate into butter/cocoa mixture, then stir in egg yolk mixture. Lightly fold in cream.

4. Pour carefully into either 8–10 small ramekins or 1 terrine/loaf tin, which you have lined with clingfilm. Tap gently to level surface, cover and chill. (For individual ramekins, it takes about 2 hours to set; for the terrine, about 3–4 hours.)

5. **For the raspberry sauce:** purée the ingredients in a blender or processor, then pass through a sieve to remove pips.

6. **For the white chocolate sauce:** gently warm most of the cream, then remove from the heat when just hot. Add the chocolate (chopped or grated), stir well, then add remaining cream and rum or Cointreau. Chill well before serving (it thickens up as it cools).

7. **To serve:** invert the ramekin (with the clingfilm lining, it comes out easily from the container) or terrine. Slice and place on large flat plate. Spoon some of each sauce around, and if you like, swirl them into each other with the tip of a knife. You can also decorate with some fresh raspberries, or a dusting of sifted cocoa.

THE MARQUISE CAN BE FROZEN; THE SAUCES ARE BETTER
NOT FROZEN

HILARY BROWN and her husband David have owned La Potinière, Gullane, since 1975. Her consistently high standards of cooking are achieved by an understated style which allows the flavour and taste of top-quality ingredients to dominate. This simple soup is an example.

Tomato and Mint Soup

SERVES 6

50 g (2 oz) butter, unsalted
225 g (8 oz) onions, peeled, finely sliced
900 g (2 lb) tomatoes, the redder the better
85 ml (3 fl oz) dry sherry
15 ml (1 tbsp) caster sugar
45 ml (3 tbsp) fresh, chopped or 20 ml (1 ½ tbsp) dried mint
seasoning

1. Melt the butter in a medium-sized saucepan. Add the onion and cook gently until softened but not coloured. Stir from time to time with a wooden spoon.

2. Add the tomatoes whole, with skins and stalks, the sherry, sugar and mint. No water is required at this stage. Stir together, cover with a lid, then simmer for 45–60 minutes. Stir occasionally.

3. Ladle the mixture into a liquidiser and blend until smooth.

4. Pour the soup through a mouli into a clean pan.

5. Stir together, then add enough water to correct the consistency. Season to taste, about 5–10 ml (1–2 tsp) salt. It should have plenty of body, so do not add too much water. The tomatoes should have created enough liquid.

6. Reheat the soup when wishing to serve, and ladle into warmed soup bowls or one large tureen. Garnish with a little whipped cream, topped with a sprig of mint.

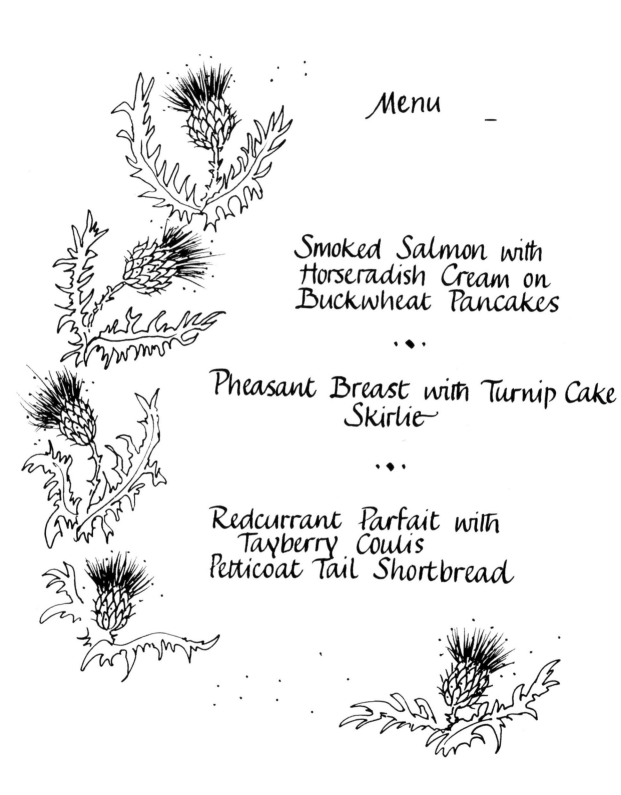

Menu

Smoked Salmon with
Horseradish Cream on
Buckwheat Pancakes

· · ·

Pheasant Breast with Turnip Cake
Skirlie

· · ·

Redcurrant Parfait with
Tayberry Coulis
Petticoat Tail Shortbread

Chapter Ten

HERE IS ANOTHER MENU OF REVAMPED CLASSICS – SMOKED SALMON, pheasant and berries. None are served in a traditional manner, but all are prepared simply and quickly, in order to let the fine natural flavours dominate. The smoked salmon is combined with little buckwheat pancakes, reminiscent of girdle (or Scotch) pancakes. The nutty, smoky flavour of buckwheat flour is perfect with the distinctive flavour of the smoked fish. Although these are not blinis (yeast-raised pancakes) the Russian influence does prevail, with the addition of sour cream or, even better, smetana, which is mixed with horseradish.

Pheasant is not a particularly strongly flavoured game bird, which makes it suitable for most palates. It lends itself to a variety of accompanying sauces, from fruit to cheese, gin to claret; and to various methods of cooking, from quick roasting for young birds, to casseroling for the more elderly. It is important to bear in mind that pheasant meat has a tendency to dry out, so smothering with bacon or other fat, or frequent basting, is recommended. My recipe demands that the breasts alone be roasted quickly in a very hot oven; the carcass is ideal for the stock for your sauce. Whisky adds an extra dimension to the sauce – and a taste of Scotland which marries well with the indigenous game. The turnip cake is similar in cooking technique to a *gratin dauphinois*, but it is made primarily with turnip (swede) and served in a cake-like slice. The deeper the tin you use to cook it, the more impressive it looks on the plate: height is important, visually, in presentation. Skirlie is a traditional Scottish accompaniment to game, roast meat or, more commonly, mince and tatties. Its ingredients are the same as white (mealie) puddings, which are boiled, as opposed to fried. Skirlie is useful as a stuffing or as an accompaniment to game, rather like fried breadcrumbs; I personally prefer the nutty oatmeal taste to the breadcrumbs, but that could be national prejudice.

The redcurrants in the parfait can be interchanged with other berries, such as blackcurrants or cranberries; the sugar content should be altered according to taste. It looks beautiful served in individual ramekins or sliced from a terrine and with the tayberry sauce poured around. Tayberries are a hybrid of raspberries and brambles (blackberries). My local fruit farm (where I drag the family to 'pick-your-own' every summer) have tayberries for sale and their popularity is on the increase. Since they have a long stalk which can be difficult to remove, the sauce recipe simplifies matters by sieving at the end, to remove pips and stalks. Raspberries are the best alternative, if tayberries are unobtainable.

THE BUCKWHEAT PANCAKES CAN BE MADE ON THE DAY AND REHEATED. PUT THEM IN A MODERATE OVEN, WRAPPED IN A FOIL PARCEL WITH A LITTLE MELTED BUTTER. THE TURNIP CAKE IS EASIER TO CUT IF MADE THE NIGHT BEFORE AND REFRIGERATED. THE PUDDING SHOULD BE FROZEN IN ADVANCE, BUT ITS SAUCE MADE ON THE DAY

Smoked salmon and champagne are a perfect combination, so for the starter, go bubbly. If you cannot afford the real thing, a sparkling Saumur would be fine. Any good-quality red wine – a fine Burgundy, for example – is good with pheasant. I would recommend more fizz for the pudding – but sweeter – Asti Spumante, or even sparkling mineral water.

Smoked Salmon with Horseradish Cream on Buckwheat Pancakes

PANCAKES

100 g (4 oz) plain flour
50 g (2 oz) buckwheat flour
150 ml (5 fl oz) milk
75 ml (5 tbsp) water
2 ml (½ tsp) caster sugar
15 g (½ oz) butter
1 ml (¼ tsp) salt
1 large egg, separated
(butter to fry)

TOPPING

50–75 g (2–3 oz) piece smoked salmon fillet
(preferably not pre-sliced)
5–10 ml (1–2 tsp) freshly grated horseradish
(or best-quality relish)
150 ml (5 fl oz) soured cream (or smetana)
lemon juice

TO FINISH

fresh chives, snipped

1. **For pancakes:** place milk, water, sugar and butter in a saucepan and heat gently until butter melts. Pour into food processor and add the sifted flours, salt and egg yolk. Blend to a smooth batter then transfer to a bowl for 1–1½ hours until frothy. Whisk egg white until soft peaks form, then fold into the batter.

2. Cut salmon into diagonal slices (or, if already sliced, curl up loosely). Sprinkle with lemon juice. Mix the horseradish with the soured cream (season, if necessary).

3. **To cook pancakes:** heat a heavy-based frying pan until very hot. Grease with a minimum of melted butter, then drop dessert-spoonfuls of batter into the pan, spacing well apart. Cook for about a minute then, when tiny bubbles appear, flip pancake over and cook on other side until brown. Wrap pancakes in loose foil parcel and keep warm in moderate oven, while cooking the remainder.

4. **To serve:** place 3 pancakes on individual plates, top with some horseradish cream then the salmon. Sprinkle liberally with chives. (These are also superb served with drinks – preferably champagne! – in which case, spoon batter with a teaspoon, for smaller pancakes.)

THE BUCKWHEAT PANCAKES FREEZE WELL; REHEAT IN A FOIL PARCEL, IN MODERATE OVEN

Pheasant Breast with Turnip Cake

PHEASANT

4 pheasant breasts, taken from young birds (use carcass for stock for sauce)
15 ml (1 tbsp) olive oil
15 ml (1 tbsp) hazelnut oil
15 g (½ oz) butter

SAUCE

300 ml (10 fl oz) reduced pheasant stock
30 ml (2 tbsp) whisky
salt, ground pepper

1. Remove skin from breasts and cover with oils (pressing all over with fingers). Cover with clingfilm and refrigerate for several hours.

2. Melt butter in pan, add breasts, season lightly and brown all over (1–2 minutes).

3. Remove and place on a lightly buttered baking tray. Cook in centre of preheated oven 230°C (450°F/Gas 8) for 7–8 minutes, until just cooked (check as you would for chicken, by piercing meat; if juices run clear, it is ready). Rest meat for 5 minutes.

4. **For sauce:** heat the stock with the whisky, bring to the boil then simmer for about 20 minutes until well reduced, to sauce-like consistency. Season well.

5. **To serve:** slice pheasant breast and place on plate, with a little sauce poured over. Serve a spoonful of skirlie alongside the turnip cake wedge. (A steamed green vegetable, like Savoy cabbage, could also be offered.)

TURNIP CAKE

450 g (1 lb) (peeled weight) turnip (swede)
225 g (8 oz) (peeled weight) potato
2 cloves garlic, peeled, crushed
grating of nutmeg
7 ml (1 ½ tsp) salt
freshly ground pepper
125 ml (4 fl oz) milk
175 ml (6 fl oz) double cream
15 g (½ oz) butter

1. Peel vegetables and slice finely (it is easiest in the food processor, with the slicing blade).

2. Place vegetables in a large pan with the milk, cream, salt and garlic. Bring to the boil then reduce the heat and stir occasionally.

3. Cook for about 5 minutes or until thickened slightly. Season well with pepper and a little nutmeg.

4. Pour into a well-buttered round, deep dish about 18 cm (7 inches). Dot with butter over the top and bake in a preheated oven 180°C (350°F/Gas 4) for about 1¼ hours, until vegetables are tender. (Cover with foil for the last 30 minutes.)

5. Either serve immediately, as a whole, or – even better – allow to cool, then refrigerate overnight. Next day, carefully cut out cake-like wedges, place on a buttered baking tray and reheat for 8 minutes under the pheasant.

Skirlie

50–75 g (2–3 oz) butter/olive oil/dripping
1 large onion, peeled, chopped finely
100 g (4 oz) medium oatmeal
30 ml (2 tbsp) freshly chopped parsley

1. Fry the onion in the hot fat (for about 5 minutes).

2. Add the oatmeal and stir until toasted and crumbly (about 5–10 minutes). Season well.
(This can be reheated, covered in foil, under the pheasant, for 5–10 minutes.) Serve with pheasant, and sprinkle liberally with parsley.

NONE OF THE MAIN COURSE CAN BE FROZEN, APART FROM
STOCK FOR THE SAUCE

CHOCOLATE MARQUISE WITH TWO SAUCES

PHEASANT BREAST WITH TURNIP CAKE AND SKIRLIE

Redcurrant Parfait with Tayberry Coulis

REDCURRANT PARFAIT

450 g (1 lb) redcurrants
100 g (4 oz) icing sugar, sifted
2 egg yolks
150 ml (5 fl oz) double or whipping cream, lightly whipped

TAYBERRY COULIS

325 g (12 oz) tayberries (or half raspberries, half brambles)
50–75 g (2–3 oz) icing sugar, sifted
juice of 1 lemon
dash of gin

1. After reserving a few redcurrants for decoration, place the remainder in a saucepan with 30 ml (2 tbsp) water. Bring to the boil and simmer for about 5 minutes until soft. Drain.

2. Purée in food processor, then sieve.

3. Whisk egg yolks with sugar until frothy, then add to the redcurrant purée. Fold in cream.

4. Turn into 4 small ramekins and freeze. Remove from freezer 10 minutes before serving, and dip outside of ramekins in hot water, run knife round and invert on to plate. Serve with a pool of the coulis and some shortbread.

5. **For coulis:** place all ingredients in a food processor and blend until smooth. Pass through a sieve, taste and add more sugar if required. Chill well.

Petticoat Tail Shortbread

175 g (6 oz) slightly salted butter, softened
50 g (2 oz) caster sugar
175 g (6 oz) plain flour, sifted
50 g (2 oz) Farola (fine semolina)
caster sugar

1. Cream butter and sugar together until light and fluffy. Sift in flour with the Farola, mix through, then knead very briefly (over-handling makes it tough).

2. Divide into 3 pieces and lightly press each into a buttered 15 cm (6 inch) (fluted) sandwich tin. Prick all over with a fork.

3. Bake in preheated oven 150°C (300°F/Gas 2) for 35–40 minutes, or until golden.

4. Mark the shortbread into wedges immediately, sprinkle with caster sugar and cool before removing from tin.

THE PARFAIT MUST BE FROZEN. ALTHOUGH IT IS NOT ADVIS-
ABLE TO FREEZE THE COULIS, THE SHORTBREAD FREEZES
WELL (IF THERE IS ANY LEFT!)

FERRIER RICHARDSON of October Restaurant, Bearsden, Glasgow, is a young, creative chef whose roots are traditionally Scottish, yet who looks not only to his own country but abroad – to Italy, Japan, Australia – for inspiration.

Trio of Summer Fruits

SERVES 6

Hot Raspberry Soufflé

500 ml (16 fl oz) milk
520 g (18 oz) sugar
6 egg yolks
50 g (2 oz) flour
30 g (1 oz) butter
1.1 kg (2 ½ lb) raspberries, fresh or frozen
30 ml (2 tbsp) framboise eau-de-vie
1 litre (1 ½ pints) water
juice of 1 lemon
60 g (2 ½ oz) butter, melted
10 egg whites
50 g (2 oz) icing sugar, to serve

1. Preheat oven to 220°C (425°F/Gas 7).

2. Place milk and 80 g (3 oz) sugar in a saucepan and bring to the boil. Place the egg yolks in a bowl, add 45 g (2 oz) sugar and beat straight away with a wire whisk for several minutes. At this point, stir in the flour until the mixture is smooth, pour on the boiling milk, whisking continuously.

3. Pour the custard mixture back into the pan, place on a high heat and boil for approximately 3 minutes, stirring continuously. Flake 30 g (1 oz) butter and dot at intervals over the surface to stop a skin forming; keep in a warm place.

4. Place approximately 18 raspberries in a bowl with 15 ml (1 tbsp) framboise. Cover and lay aside. Place the rest of the raspberries in a saucepan with 300 g (11 oz) sugar and the water. Place on a high heat to boil and cook for about 5 minutes.

5. This mixture should then be puréed and passed through a sieve.

6. Separate two-thirds of the mixture and place back in pan; place on a high heat and cook gently until it has the consistency of jam. Leave aside. Then add lemon juice to the remaining framboise and purée: this will make a coulis; keep warm in a bain-marie.

7. Brush 6 small soufflé ramekins with the melted butter and then coat each dish with sugar, about 70 g (3 oz). Fold the raspberry jam mixture into the custard and pour this into another bowl. Now beat the egg whites until slightly foamy, then add 25 g (1 oz) sugar and continue beating until soft peaks form. Using a wire whisk, speedily mix one-third of the egg whites into the custard and then gently fold in the rest of the egg whites. Fill each ramekin with half the soufflé mixture, then add 3-4 of the preserved raspberries and then the remaining soufflé mixture.

8. Smooth each soufflé to make level and push mixture away from the sides of the dish with the point of a knife. Place in preheated oven for 8-10 minutes. Before serving, dust soufflés with icing sugar and serve with the raspberry coulis (warm) in a small jug next to the tart and sorbet.

Strawberry Tart

200 g (7 oz) flour
50 g (2 oz) ground almonds
100 g (4 oz) unsalted butter
75 g (3 oz) icing sugar
1 egg yolk
15 ml (1 tbsp) milk
300 ml (10 fl oz) double cream
1 punnet strawberries
75 ml (3 fl oz) strawberry glaze
bunch of fresh mint

1. Preheat oven to 200°C (400°F/Gas 6).

2. Make shortcrust pastry from the flour, almonds, butter, icing sugar and milk. (For fuller instructions see p125.) Chill well before rolling out to approximately 5 mm (¼ inch) thickness. Line fluted tartlet moulds with the pastry and bake blind in the preheated oven.

3. Whip the double cream until soft peaks form. Place cream in a piping bag and pipe on to the pastry bases in a tall cone shape. Halve the fresh strawberries and place on to the cream all the way round. Cover these with the glaze and decorate with pieces of fresh mint. Place on plate next to soufflé and sorbet.

Blackcurrant Sorbet

750 ml (25 fl oz) blackcurrant pulp
juice of 1 lemon
500 ml (16 fl oz) sorbet syrup

SORBET SYRUP

50 g (2 oz) sugar
650 ml (22 fl oz) water
90 g (4 oz) glucose

1. **For sorbet syrup:** place all ingredients in a saucepan and bring to the boil, stirring occasionally with a wooden spoon. Boil for approximately 3 minutes, skimming mixture if required.

2. Pass syrup through a strainer and leave until cold before using in the recipe.

3. Pass blackcurrants through sieve or conical strainer into a bowl. Add sorbet syrup (as much as you need, depending on sweetness of fruit). If the mixture is not ripe enough, add lemon juice to enhance flavour. Pour mixture into ice-cream maker and churn for 10–20 minutes, depending on machine.

4. Serve the sorbet immediately on plate next to tart and soufflé.

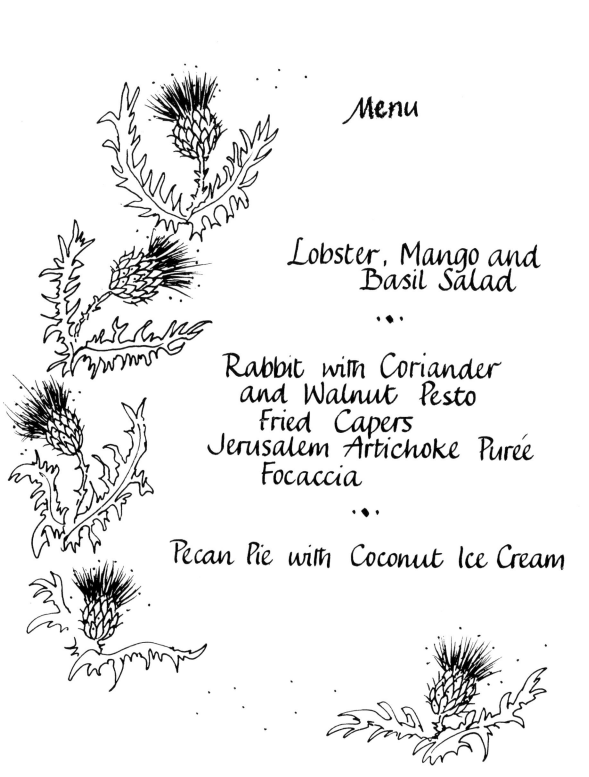

Menu

Lobster, Mango and
Basil Salad

...

Rabbit with Coriander
and Walnut Pesto
Fried Capers
Jerusalem Artichoke Purée
Focaccia

...

Pecan Pie with Coconut Ice Cream

Chapter Eleven

THIS IS NOT A MENU FOR THE FAINT-HEARTED. THE ROBUST FLAVOUR of the dishes can be an acquired taste. Personally I love the intensity of the flavours – lobster, basil, coriander, capers and a rather liberal application of finest olive oil.

The combination of mango with lobster harks back to my three-month stay in Australia, where lobsters are so much cheaper than here; no special occasion was needed to indulge in these splendid crustaceans. Not only do the flavours of the starter blend well, but so do the textures. These are enhanced by the aromatic flavour of fresh basil in the dressing, which also adds a good colour contrast. If you cannot bear to cook the live lobster yourself, ask your fishmonger; mine will cook them to order, so it is still warm – and perfectly cooked – when sold. Since lobsters in Britain are expensive (unjustifiably, since Scotland's catch of shellfish is plentiful) the starter is the most costly course. This is balanced by one of the cheapest of all meats, rabbit.

The rabbit joints are smothered in a pesto sauce made not from basil, Parmesan and pinenuts, but from coriander, Pecorino and walnuts. It is a superb combination and a versatile one – other fresh herbs or nuts can be used depending on availability. Rabbit used to be eaten very frequently in Scotland: my mother remembers the cast-iron pot on the cooking range filled with warming rabbit stew. It combines well with strong flavours like mustard or my powerful coriander sauce. Chicken breasts also go well with the pesto. The Jerusalem artichoke purée is redolent of fine olive oil, which enhances the deli-cate flavour of this knobbly tuber. Focaccia is an Italian olive oil bread which I make with Italian OO flour and fresh rosemary. If you can obtain rosemary flowers, their colour and fragrance are ideal as a garnish. The flowers of strongly flavoured herbs, such as chive, mint, rosemary, often have a more delicate version of the herb's flavour. They are, therefore, perfect in salads, drinks or as decoration.

Pecan pie (along with blueberry pie) is surely the archetypal American pie. Mine does resemble the rich sweet pie of the States, but with the addition of lemon zest and juice, the end result is less sickly sweet, and quite delicious. Walnuts or raw Macadamia nuts (which are indigenous to Australia) are also suitable alternatives. The coconut ice-cream compounds the nutty theme of the pudding – and indulges my passion for nuts of all sorts. However, if you prefer, a good vanilla or Cornish ice-cream would also go well.

THE LOBSTER CAN BE BOILED EARLIER ON THE DAY AND THE DRESSING PREPARED IN ADVANCE. THE CORIANDER PESTO LASTS FOR WEEKS IN THE FRIDGE. THE PURÉE AND FOCACCIA ARE BEST MADE ON THE DAY. THE PECAN PIE CAN BE MADE EARLIER IN THE DAY AND REHEATED. THE ICE-CREAM CAN BE MADE A DAY OR TWO IN ADVANCE

Alsace Riesling or Mosel Spatlese are both good to drink with the starter, while a young Italian red or a Rhône rosé match any rabbit dish well. A glass of finest Madeira slips down very easily with the wickedly rich pudding.

Lobster, Mango and Basil Salad

SALAD

1 freshly boiled lobster, about 700 g (1 ½ lb);
more if you feel wealthy!
1 large ripe mango, peeled, cut into chunks
(about same size as lobster slices)
1 frisée lettuce, prepared
handful of fresh basil leaves

DRESSING

45 ml (3 tbsp) olive oil
15 ml (1 tbsp) wine or cider vinegar
salt, pepper
5–10 ml (1–2 tsp) pesto sauce

1. Remove head, claws and shell from lobster (like peeling a large prawn). Cut the body flesh into thick slices. Crack claws but leave whole.

2. Mix all dressing ingredients together.

3. Place lobster meat and mango chunks in a bowl, pour over dressing and carefully coat all over.

4. Shred basil leaves at the last moment and add.

5. Line a large flat bowl with the frisée lettuce and pour in the salad. Garnish with the lobster claws and basil sprigs. (I usually serve the first batch of focaccia with this, to mop up the basil/oily dressing.)

NONE OF THE STARTER CAN BE FROZEN

Rabbit with Coriander and Walnut Pesto

RABBIT

900 g (2 lb) young rabbit, jointed (about 2 good-size joints each)
olive oil
salt, ground pepper

PESTO

2 large handfuls coriander leaves
50 g (2 oz) walnut pieces
50 g (2 oz) green pumpkin seeds
(available from health-food shops)
2–3 cloves garlic, crushed
30 ml (2 tbsp) fresh lime juice
100 g (4 oz) Pecorino cheese (Parmesan will do), freshly grated
5 ml (1 tsp) salt
freshly ground pepper
100–150 ml (4–5 fl oz) extra virgin olive oil

1. **For pesto:** place all ingredients (except oil) in food processor and blend well, slowly adding sufficient oil until thick coating sauce consistency is achieved. Taste to check seasoning. (If not using all of this, it lasts well in the fridge to mix into pasta sauces or vegetables, stored in a screw-top jar.)

2. **For rabbit:** rub olive oil all over rabbit and place on oiled baking tray. Season then spread a layer of the pesto on top. Cover tightly with oiled foil.·

3. Place in middle of preheated oven 200°C (400°F/Gas 6) for 25–30 minutes. Remove foil and bake uncovered for a further 5 minutes. Serve with fried capers sprinkled over the top.

Fried Capers

50–75 g (2–3 oz) capers (preferably loose from a delicatessen; they
are usually plumper)
olive oil
balsamic vinegar

1. Rinse off excess salt, pat dry well with kitchen paper.

2. Heat some oil in a pan and fry the capers on a high heat until
   crisp. Remove from heat and add a splash of balsamic vinegar,
   tossing through. Serve at once over rabbit.

Jerusalem Artichoke Purée

1.4 kg (3 lb) Jerusalem artichokes, peeled
40 g (1 ½ oz) unsalted butter
45 ml (3 tbsp) extra virgin olive oil
salt, freshly ground pepper

1. Place artichokes (cut into pieces if large) in pot with cold water,
   bring to boil and simmer for 15–20 minutes until tender.

2. Drain well and place hot artichokes into a food processor with the
   butter. Process briefly then, with motor running, slowly pour in
   oil. Season to taste, pour into bowl and drizzle some olive oil over
   top at last minute.

Focaccia

225 g (8 oz) Italian OO flour (or strong white flour, but flavour
will not be as authentic)
15 g (½ oz) fresh yeast. If using dried yeast,
follow instructions on packet
pinch of sugar
2.5 ml (½ tsp) salt
150–175 ml (5–6 fl oz) lukewarm water
15 ml (1 tbsp) olive oil
olive oil, to brush (even better, rosemary-flavoured olive oil)
coarse sea salt
handful of rosemary leaves

1. Sift the flour and salt into a bowl. Dissolve yeast with sugar in a little of the lukewarm water and leave until frothy (about 10 minutes).

2. Pour on to the flour, add the olive oil and enough water to bind to a soft dough. Knead for about 10 minutes, roll in a little oil, cover and leave to rise for about 1 hour in a warm place.

3. Knock back the dough, knead briefly and shape into a round about 1 cm (½ inch) thick. (Try not to use a rolling pin, but ease out with the palms of your hands.)

4. Place this on an oiled baking sheet, make dimples all over with your knuckles and sprinkle liberally with rosemary-flavoured (or normal) olive oil. Sprinkle a little coarse salt over the top. Put a few rosemary leaves into each dimple, then let it rise in a warm place for about 20 minutes. (There is no need to cover; it will not dry out, with the oil on top.)

5. Bake in a preheated oven 230°C (450°F/Gas 8) for about 20 minutes until puffed up and golden. Brush immediately with rosemary-flavoured oil and serve warm (decorated with rosemary flowers if you are lucky enough to have them).

THE PESTO CAN BE FROZEN SUCCESSFULLY, BUT NOT FOR
TOO LONG, AS THE GARLIC BECOMES TOO PUNGENT. THE
FOCACCIA FREEZES WELL AND SHOULD BE DEFROSTED AND
WARMED IN FOIL IN THE OVEN

Pecan Pie with Coconut Ice-cream

PASTRY

100 g (4 oz) plain flour
pinch of salt
50 g (2 oz) caster sugar
50 g (2 oz) ground almonds
75 g (3 oz) unsalted butter
juice of ½ lemon
1 egg yolk

FILLING

3 eggs, medium
50 g (2 oz) light muscovado sugar
100 g (4 oz) unsalted butter, melted
100 g (4 oz) golden syrup
finely grated rind and juice of 1 large lemon
200 g (7 oz) shelled pecan nuts

1. **For pastry:** sift the flour and salt into a food processor. Add the caster sugar and ground almonds and process briefly. Add the butter, cubed, and process until mixture resembles breadcrumbs. Add the lemon juice and egg yolk and process briefly until the dough 'balls'. Wrap in clingfilm and leave to rest in fridge for about 1 hour.

2. Roll out the pastry thinly on lightly floured board and line a buttered loose-bottomed 20 cm (8 inch) flan tin. Prick lightly then rest in fridge (overnight is best, to avoid any shrinkage; 1 hour will do).

3. Line with foil and baking beans and bake blind in preheated oven 200°C (400°F/Gas 6) for 15 minutes. Remove foil and beans and bake for a further 5–10 minutes until just cooked.

4. **For filling:** beat eggs with muscovado sugar, butter and syrup until smooth. Stir in the lemon rind and juice. Roughly chop most of the nuts, leaving about 6 whole. Place broken ones in pastry case, then pour over filling. Place reserved nuts round edges. Bake in preheated oven 180°C (350°F/Gas 4) for about 35–45 minutes, or until just set. Remove when cooled, as the pastry is fragile. Serve in wedges with the coconut ice-cream.

COCONUT ICE-CREAM

100 g (4 oz) desiccated coconut
250 ml (9 fl oz) double cream
250 ml (9 fl oz) milk
100 g (4 oz) jaggery (coconut palm sugar, available from specialist Indian shops; dark muscovado sugar will do)
6 egg yolks

1. Heat the cream, milk, coconut and jaggery over a low heat until just simmering. Remove from heat, cover and allow to stand for about 1 hour, to allow flavours to develop.

2. Strain through a fine sieve, discarding solids. Beat egg yolks and gradually pour in the cream mixture.

3. Place, either in heat-proof bowl over a saucepan of simmering water, or in a heavy-based reliable pan (copper is good for custards, although expensive). Stir over a low heat until the mixture coats the back of a wooden spoon. Remove from the heat and cool completely (I press clingfilm on to the surface to avoid a skin forming).

4. Pour into an ice-cream machine (or freezerproof bowl, whisking every 30 minutes until frozen) for about 30 minutes, until well churned and thick. Serve with the pecan pie.

THE PIE FREEZES WELL; THAW COMPLETELY BEFORE REHEATING IN MEDIUM OVEN FOR 15 MINUTES.

ANDREW RADFORD, chef at Waterloo Place, Edinburgh, is young, imaginative and completely self-taught. He cooks with confidence, in a style which combines ingredients with a sense of freedom, which is sometimes lacking in classically trained chefs. He shares a nutty pudding with us.

Photograph © *The Scotsman*

Bitter Chocolate Mousse with Pistachio and Hazelnut Praline, layered with Shortbread

SERVES 10

CHOCOLATE MOUSSE

325 g (12 oz) bitter chocolate
6 eggs, separated
60 ml (4 tbsp) Grand Marnier
65 g (2 ½ oz) butter

CARAMEL SAUCE

175 g (6 oz) sugar
225 ml (8 fl oz) water

PRALINE

100 g (4 oz) sugar
125 ml (4 fl oz) water
175 g (6 oz) shelled pistachios and hazelnuts

TO FINISH

20 x 10 cm (4 inch) (round) shortbread thins

1. **For praline:** boil the sugar and water together and cook until a dark amber colour. Place nuts on a greased baking tray and pour over the caramel and allow to cool. Break up the 'toffee' and grind in a mixer until a coarse powder results.

2. **For mousse:** melt chocolate and butter together. Mix the egg yolks with the Grand Marnier, then add this to the melted chocolate and butter. Whisk the egg whites to peak and carefully fold one-third into the chocolate mixture; then fold in the praline. Fold in the remaining egg whites. Pour into clean bowl and refrigerate.

3. **For caramel sauce:** bring the sugar and 175 ml (6 fl oz) water to the boil and cook until a dark amber colour. Remove from heat and carefully add to this the remaining water. Cool.

4. **To assemble:** on each of 10 chilled large plates, place one short-bread thin. Place a scoop of mousse on top. Position the second shortbread thin on top, then pour a little caramel sauce to the front. Serve immediately.

RABBIT WITH CORIANDER AND WALNUT PESTO, CAPERS,
JERUSALEM ARTICHOKE PURÉE AND FOCACCIA

7-CUP PUDDING WITH BUTTERSCOTCH SAUCE AND CRÈME
FRAÎCHE

Chapter Twelve

THE DISHES IN THIS MENU ARE OF TRADITIONAL DERIVATION. My recipes, however, deviate from the norm with the addition of rather atypical ingredients.

The soup is not the regular cock-a-leekie, which has prunes chopped into it. The basic components – chicken and leeks – are still present, but, instead of prunes, I have substituted slivers of avocado, which combine naturally with chicken (a delicious sandwich filling is avocado, chicken and mayonnaise). It is a light clear soup, therefore ideal before the next courses, especially the rich pudding.

Scottish salmon is famous worldwide. Apart from its magnificent flavour and texture, the colour is splendid, especially on plain white plates. Green seems to match its pink hue well, and the fish is often served with watercress, dill or, in this case, spinach and sorrel. Salmon has a tendency to dry out quickly, so try to avoid overcooking. I always aim to undercook, testing as I go; it can always be flashed under the grill for another minute if necessary. The skin is delicious to eat when cooked in this way, as it is crispy and contrasts well with the succulent, moist flesh. The wild salmon season in Scotland is from February to September. Farmed salmon has the advantage of being cheaper and available all year, although some experts believe the flavour is not comparable.

Fresh lemon grass, widely used in South-Asian cooking, is aromatic and 'citrusy'. For the sauce, the stems should be bruised or cut roughly to impart the flavour (it will later be strained). If it is to be eaten in a dish, the lower half of the stem should be finely chopped, having removed the tough outer layer. Dried lemon grass should always be soaked in water, wine or stock, before use. A light salad of young spinach and slighty bitter-tasting sorrel accompanies the creamy lemon grass sauce with the salmon. Sorrel, like basil, responds better to tearing or shredding, rather than cutting with a knife; only young, tender leaves should be used.

Menu

Cock - a - Leekie with Avocado

• • •

Salmon with Lemon Grass
Spinach & Sorrel Salad

• • •

7 - cup Pudding with
Butterscotch Sauce & Crème Fraîche

The pudding is a triumph. It is a hot, steamed fruit pudding with a sweet butterscotch sauce and refreshing crème fraîche, based on the traditional Scottish pudding, Cloutie Dumpling. My recipe is more straightforward, since it is steamed in a bowl, not in a 'clout', or cloth. The 'skin' of the authentic dumpling, which forms on the outside of the pudding, is the only element missing from my version. In my parents' childhood, after it was steamed and removed from its 'clout', the dumpling was placed on a plate on a stool in front of the open fire-place. My mother's task used to be to keep turning the dumpling round, for about 15 minutes, until the sticky skin dried off. Cloutie dumplings were made regulary for birthdays – certainly in Dundee, where birthday cakes were rare. Silver coins were often added, like charms in Christmas puddings. My aunt still makes a splendid dumpling for each member of the family's birthday. Usually served on the day with custard, it would be fried the next day in rendered suet and eaten with bacon.

Over the sea, in Holland, 'Jan in de Zak' is the Dutch equivalent – a rich fruit pudding, boiled in a cloth or pillowcase. The father of my Dutch friend Mary-An, who owns a garden centre, makes one in an (unused!) bulb sack, to suit his very large family. My 7-Cup pudding should be served in small slices, with butterscotch sauce and the crème fraîche – its acidic taste is perfect to cut through the sweetness of the sauce and pudding.

THE STOCK FOR THE SOUP CAN BE MADE IN ADVANCE, AS CAN THE FISH STOCK FOR THE SAUCE. THE SALAD DRESSING AND BUTTERSCOTCH SAUCE CAN ALSO BE PREPARED EARLIER. THE OTHER ITEMS REQUIRE LAST-MINUTE ATTENTION.

A Sancerre or Australian Chardonnay are good accompaniments to the soup. The exquisite taste of the salmon deserves the best: if you can afford it, serve a Chablis Grand Cru. Otherwise, for a less expensive alternative, try a Californian Riesling. The pudding is very rich – a still mineral water will suffice, or a glass of Tawny Port for the trenchermen.

Cock-a-leekie with Avocado

1 large raw chicken breast, about 225 g (8 oz), skinned, boned
900 ml (30 fl oz) rich chicken stock (strained through muslin and
degreased)
225 g (8 oz) leeks, trimmed, washed, cut into thin slices
1 large ripe avocado, peeled, sliced
salt, pepper
25 g (1 oz) unsalted butter
freshly chopped parsley or chives

1. Melt butter in pan. Cut chicken into thin strips and add. Cook gently in butter for 3–4 minutes.

2. Remove with slotted spoon and keep warm.

3. Put leeks into a pan, sauté for about 5 minutes, stirring occasionally.

4. Pour in the stock, reheat, season to taste.

5. Place 2–3 slices of avocado in each warmed soup bowl, top with some chicken strips, then the leek soup.

6. Sprinkle over the parsley and serve at once.

THE STOCK CAN BE FROZEN.

Salmon with Lemon Grass Sauce

SALMON

4 salmon fillets, boneless (about 100–175 g (4–6 oz))
40 g (1 ½ oz) butter, softened
15 ml (1 tbsp) olive oil
sea salt, freshly ground pepper

SAUCE

25 g (1 oz) shallots, peeled, chopped
olive oil
200 ml (7 fl oz) white wine
200 ml (7 fl oz) reduced fish stock
150 ml (5 fl oz) double cream
salt, ground pepper
50 g (2 oz) unsalted butter, cubed
25 g (1 oz) fresh lemon grass (or 5 ml (1 tsp) dried, soaked in
15 ml (1 tbsp) white wine)

1. **For the sauce:** sauté the shallots in oil until golden, then add the wine and stock. Remove the outer layer of the lemon grass, bruise or roughly chop and add to the pan (or add dried lemon grass soaked in wine). Bring to the boil and reduce by half.

2. Stir in the cream and bring to the boil. Simmer and reduce until sauce-like consistency.

3. Strain through a fine sieve then return to the pan, season and whisk in the butter, a little at a time. For a more frothy effect, whirl it in the food processor. Keep warm while you tackle the salmon.

4. **For the salmon:** make sure it is well-scaled (since the skin can be eaten). Season well, slash the skin in two places and rub the softened (or melted and cooled) butter with the olive oil all over.

5. Place in a flat grill-proof dish, skin-side underneath. If you refrigerate at this point (for up to 6 hours), bring it back to room temperature.

6. Place under preheated, very hot grill (I put mine on at least 15 minutes prior to using) for 2 minutes. Then turn the fillets, so they are skin-side up, and grill for a further 2 minutes. Remove, test if the fish is cooked with the point of a knife and serve at once with the lemon grass sauce. (I pour the sauce around, not on top of the fish otherwise you will spoil the lovely crispy skin.)

Spinach and Sorrel Salad

700 g (1 ½ lb) young spinach leaves
75–100 g (3–4 oz) young sorrel leaves
palm hearts (if obtainable)
15 ml (1 tbsp) balsamic or sherry vinegar
60–75 ml (4–5 tbsp) olive oil and walnut or pine-kernel oil, mixed
2 ml (½ tsp) Dijon mustard
salt, freshly ground pepper

1. Prepare spinach and sorrel by removing any coarse stalks, washing and drying well, and tearing roughly into a large salad bowl.

2. **For dressing:** mix the vinegar with the mustard, season then add enough nut and olive oils to give a thick emulsion.

3. Pour over the salad (just enough to coat each leaf) and toss well at the last minute. (If you can get hold of tinned palm hearts – Palmitos – cut these into thin slices and add to the salad; their texture provides a pleasant contrast with the spinach; a lime dressing is also good with them.)

THE FISH STOCK CAN BE FROZEN; EVERYTHING ELSE MUST BE DONE AT THE LAST MINUTE.

7-Cup Pudding
with Butterscotch Sauce
and Crème Fraîche

7-CUP PUDDING

(The cup I use is an American cup, which is a large teacup size or
250 ml (8 fl oz)
1 cup raisins or currants
1 cup sultanas
1 cup self-raising flour
1 cup suet
1 cup fresh breadcrumbs (I prefer brown)
1 cup soft light brown sugar
1 cup milk
1 egg, medium
5 ml (1 tsp) cinnamon
5 ml (1 tsp) mixed spice

1. Mix the first 6 cupfuls in a bowl with the spices.

2. Add the milk and beaten egg.

3. Pour into a buttered 1200 ml (2 pint) pudding bowl. Cover with a double layer of buttered foil, with a pleat across the centre. Secure with string.

4. Steam for 2½–3 hours (keep checking the water level in your steamer or pan). Turn out on to a dish and pour the butterscotch sauce over the top.

5. Place in preheated oven 200°C (400°F/Gas 6) for 3–4 minutes until the sauce bubbles (and you can wait no longer!). Serve at once in small slices, with some sauce spooned over and the crème fraîche served separately.

BUTTERSCOTCH SAUCE

75 g (3 oz) soft dark brown sugar
50 g (2 oz) unsalted butter
150 ml (5 fl oz) double cream
dash of pure vanilla essence

TO FINISH

200 ml (7 fl oz) crème fraîche

1. Place all sauce ingredients together in a pan, heat very gently until the sugar dissolves.

2. Boil for 2–3 minutes until syrupy then pour over the pudding. Offer the crème fraîche separately.

NONE OF THE PUDDING SHOULD BE FROZEN.

BETTY ALLEN, owner of Airds Hotel, Port Appin, with her husband Eric, is another self-taught chef whose cooking is among the finest in Scotland. She uses local seafood – the hotel is on the shores of Loch Linnhe – and cooks in an unpretentious manner, to bring out the natural intensity of the flavours.

Photograph © *The Scotsman*

Salmon and Halibut en croûte

SERVES 6-8

1 small egg for glaze
approx 275 g (10 oz) flaky or puff pastry
450 g (1 lb) middle cut salmon, skinned and filleted into 2 long thick steaks about 7 cm (3 inch) by 20 cm (8 inch) rubbed with lemon juice
225 g (8 oz) halibut, skinned and filleted to 1 piece, same size as salmon
100 g (4 oz) butter, softened
50 g (2 oz) jar Danish lumpfish roe
salt, freshly ground pepper
lemon wedges and fresh dill to garnish

1. Roll out the pastry as thinly as possible on a lightly floured board.

2. Place one fillet of salmon in the middle of the pastry.

3. Season it, then spread the surface with half of the butter. Spread half the roe over the butter.

4. Place the seasoned halibut over the roe, spread with butter and the remaining roe. Top with the rest of the salmon, season again and press lightly into a rectangle about 10 cm (4 inch) by 20 cm (8 inch).

5. Paint the circumference with egg wash and completely enfold the fish in pastry, pressing to seal. Trim off extra pastry.

6. Turn the parcel over to conceal the seam. Cut shapes from the trimmings and decorate the parcel.

7. Leave to rest on a baking sheet in fridge for about an hour.

8. When ready to cook, brush with egg wash, place on a hot baking sheet in a preheated oven 230°C (450°F/Gas 8) and bake for approximately 35 minutes.

9. Allow to rest in a warm place for 10 minutes before slicing into portions, using an electric knife. Garnish with lemon and dill or a thin hollandaise sauce.